It Takes a
Parent
to Raise a
Child

Also by Glen C. Griffin, M.D.

*Good Fat, Bad Fat: How to Lower Your Cholesterol and
Reduce the Odds of a Heart Attack*
(with William P. Castelli, M.D.)

It Takes a Parent to Raise a Child

9 Principles for Families to Love and Live By

Glen C. Griffin, M.D.

Golden Books
NEW YORK

Golden Books®

888 Seventh Avenue
New York, NY 10106

Designed by Gwen Petruska Gürkan

Manufactured in the United States of America

10   9   8   7   6   5   4   3   2   1

Library of Congress Cataloging-in-Publication Data

Griffin, Glen C.
    It takes a parent to raise a child: 9 principles for families
to love and live by / Glen C. Griffin.
        p.   cm.
    ISBN 1-58238-038-4
    1. Parenting.   I. Title.
    HQ755.8.G744   1999
    649'.1—dc21   98-52832
                                                  CIP

With love to my family and yours

CONTENTS

INTRODUCTION

This Book's a Game Plan— Not Psychobabble!

K ids mouth off a lot these days. You've probably noticed. They don't listen. They talk back. They want everything in sight. And while you're teaching them what's right, others are telling them:

"Have fun."

"Feel good."

"Look cool."

"Do anything you want—right now."

Instant gratification is pushed in highly effective commercials for beer, fast food, pills, and clothes, along with distorted portrayals of life on television, teaching kids to want and expect fun on demand. It doesn't take a genius to figure out that life doesn't give people everything they *want*. But kids don't know this.

Besides these conflicting messages and the example of well-known people who ignore values, some so-called experts are teaching children that all of this is okay. A colorful children's book, endorsed by a well-known columnist, tells young children how to masturbate, put on a condom, have sex, and what it's like to have an orgasm.

Some want to teach these things to children in elementary

school. Typical of this thinking, a medical journal editor wrote, "Perhaps we should add contraception to the kindergarten curriculum; unfortunately I'm not kidding." [1]

Well, I'm not kidding either and I think this is a terrible idea. When you were in kindergarten, the health lessons were probably about washing hands and brushing teeth—as they should be. When you were five years old, did you know there was such a thing as a condom, let alone what it was for?

But today, some think condoms should be handed out freely—even to children. Some think it's just fine for kids to see movies and television filled with violence and immorality. Some think it's okay for kids to have sex. Some rationalize killing third-trimester babies before they are born. Some don't place much importance on honesty. Some would have us believe we can't teach values. Some would legalize drugs.

A DECLINE INTO SLIME

I don't pretend to have all the answers. No one does. And parents have always had problems. But the problems today have multiplied. Until recently, it was unusual for children to talk back to their parents or teachers. Children and teenagers had respect for adults—at least most of them did, most of the time. But as a witness to history, I've seen a slide into slime. Respect has deteriorated into shocking disrespect.

And think what kids have learned from Bill Clinton's disgusting behavior. Even young children know he did something with a woman in the White House that wasn't right—and then lied about it. Many know all the lurid details. One confused little boy asked his father, "What did President Clinton do with that girl that upset everyone so much?" How would you have answered this seven-year-old?

Kids will get these and other wrong messages from that scan-

[1] Catherine D. DeAngelis, M.D., "Editor's Note," *Archives Pediatric Adolescent Medicine,* March 1997, 243.

dal for a long time to come: "It's okay to mess around with sex," "Everyone does it," "Some sex isn't really sex," "Everyone lies," and "Words can be redefined so you really don't need to tell the truth." As the standards of morality were lowered from these escapades, a brand-new excuse was created: "But, a president did it."

It will be mostly up to you to correct this seriously damaging information. You can do it—but it won't be easy. Think how hard it is to teach kids to tell the whole truth and nothing but the truth when they have been coached so well to twist facts and the meanings of words to say something completely different than what actually happened.

And when kids hear or read about the Clinton scandal, the images of the gross behavior will *permanently contaminate* their minds—just like they did to kids as the news first unfolded. In fact, just try to get this filth out of your own brain. It's like trying to remove India ink that's been spilled on a white carpet. The moral values in this country were bad enough before all of this. But now, correcting this and other misinformation will be even more difficult.

Wrong is wrong. And right is right. Basic values go back thousands of years. We don't have to wait for new research to figure out what's good and bad for children. Forget about the *study of the week*, filled with misinformation.

It's time you and I call things like they are.

With all the wrong messages kids receive today, sometimes even at school, no wonder so many kids mouth off and get into all kinds of trouble.

YOUR KID HAS YOU

But your child has a big advantage—you.

I'm sure you've had some discouraging moments. Maybe you've even felt like your endless efforts never work. Maybe sometimes you think it isn't worth it at all. But it is.

Even if you've had a problem with a kid talking back, not doing what he or she should, throwing temper tantrums, or irritating you in other ways, things are far from hopeless.

Even if at times you feel ineffective or are scared to death you won't know how to teach your kids not to do drugs or have casual sex, I'm confident that you are just the right person to help teach them about character—and what's right and what isn't.

VILLAGES DON'T RAISE KIDS—PARENTS DO

It takes a *parent* to raise a child.

Why?

Because it takes love.

A village can't give a child love.

Neither can an institution.

But parents can and do.

The *village,* in today's culture, has done a terrible job and has forgotten about values—at least some of the *time-tested* ones that are so important to you and me. It's clear that the *village* doesn't know how to raise your child—and is disqualified for this reason alone.

Certainly parents can, and should, reach out and get help from family members, neighbors, friends, educators, spiritual leaders, and professionals—when the help they have to offer is consistent with *time-tested* values.

But the responsibility of raising a child is that of parents and family—not society. No one should encroach upon the domain of parents. And since parents are in the position to know a child better than anyone else, they are the ones who can and must teach this youngster values and principles. It's not what someone on the school board or in a government office thinks is best for your child. It's what *you* think that's important. I'm sure you believe in character and morality—and love your child enough to think a parent needs to be in charge. You probably also believe that sometimes a parent has to say no. But even though you know these things, sometimes you wonder how to do them.

ALL OF US MAKE MISTAKES

Looking back, the guidelines in this book would have really helped us as we were raising our six children. We kind of bungled along. We did many things right, but we made some mistakes—lots of them. As a pediatrician, I kept learning as I cared for thousands of children and teenagers and counseled parents in my office, ran parenting workshops, and read letters from readers of my syndicated newspaper column.

For over four decades I've been with parents during the best and the worst of times. I've been through everything from meningitis and tuberculosis to earthquakes and drownings. I've watched kids die. I've watched parents cry. I've watched teenagers shine. I've watched others spaced out on drugs and booze. I've followed kids from their moment of birth through their growing-up years—and then watched them become parents. I've seen highly effective parents. I've watched kids rebel. I've observed complex interactions between parents and children. I've seen patterns of failure and patterns of success. Some great parents have pulled off miracles. I've seen troubled youngsters turn around. And I've seen young parents and not-so-young parents raise great families. I've also watched loving parents go through heartache.

YOU CAN OVERRIDE THE
MILQUETOAST STRATEGIES

So, how do you raise a child in this very difficult time? You've probably found that the Milquetoast strategies of the day don't work. Down-to-earth things do. What you need is a *game plan* that will help you get through the rest of this week—and the years to come. You're already doing a much better job than you think you are. You can raise your kids better than most of the experts out there ever could—even the well-intentioned professionals who teach or counsel, but who don't know much about good old-fashioned values.

ANSWERS BASED ON PRINCIPLES

The wisest parents learn what they can from the experience of others. The wisest parents avoid the mistakes others have made. The wisest parents don't allow themselves to become part of the problem. By controlling conflict instead of provoking kids, these parents pull through, realizing that if they add to conflict, their children are even more vulnerable to the negative influences that disrupt their lives.

Most of these wise parents go through tough days and nights, just like all parents do. But no matter how bad the tragedy, or how tough the challenge, these parents make it. They weather the storms.

Besides the challenges parents have always faced, children and teenagers today are coached daily to defy parents and society. Every day, youngsters run through traps as dangerous as minefields.

But I have confidence in parents. Specifically, I have confidence in you. I know you can be a strong leader for your children. In the time we spend together, I'm going to share nine keys with you that I've seen help thousands of parents. They didn't hit me all at once. These keys that seem so simple took years of observing, because it takes a long time to see patterns unfold.

And these keys will help you teach your children the universal "rules of life" that have been with us throughout history. Basically, you know the *rules of life*—the principles that make up character, like *respect others, be someone everyone can trust,* and *don't do destructive things.* These and the other "rules of life" are the traditional values and principles you learned over the years at home, at school, and where you worship. They are not my rules. I'm not asking you to agree with my conclusions. I'm just asking you to accept what has stood the test of time. And quite simply, if kids follow the *rules of life* they will do pretty well. If they don't, they will make themselves and everyone around them just plain miserable. I guess I've known this for a long time, just as you do. I just didn't know how to put it all together as well as I would have liked while our kids were growing up.

THIS GAME PLAN CONSISTS OF
NINE SIMPLE PLAYS, OR KEYS

But how do you teach these time-tested principles in the midst of so much misinformation? It's tougher than facing the number one football team in the country. Nothing could be more difficult.

But suppose you were a football coach and someone handed you a *playbook* with a nine-key plan of how to win next week's game? This little book is that kind of playbook, except that it's one for the game of life with your kids. I just wish someone else had written it a long time ago and had given it to my wife and me while our children were growing up.

So sit back—and see how many things you're already doing right—and how much better things will go in your family as you use all nine keys in this game-plan playbook.

1

Take Charge As a Friend—
Not the Enemy

"How can I get my kids to do everything I want?" you may wish and wonder. Well, this isn't going to happen—ever. You know that. There is no way that you or I, or anyone else, can get children to do *everything* we want. But we will have a much better chance of getting positive results if our kids think we are their friend instead of their enemy. This means having fun together, doing lots of listening, talking softly and slowly, and teaching them stuff they won't learn from anyone else.

GAIN YOUR CHILD'S TRUST

Parenting should be more like leading sheep than herding cattle. If you haven't seen cowboys drive cattle into a corral in real life, you probably have in the movies. But you may not have seen sheep being led in and out of a sheepfold. At day's end in the Middle East, several shepherds lead their flocks of sheep into a common sheepfold for the night. Then, in the predawn hours, one shepherd at a time calls his sheep. Astonishingly, the sheep recognize their own shepherd's voice and follow him out of the sheepfold.

Cattle are driven. Sheep are led by someone they trust. How nice it would be if our children followed us as lambs follow a shepherd.

Unfortunately, when we don't know how to lead children, we end up trying to drive them—like cattle—and they often want to show their independence by going in other directions. To make matters worse, children today are programmed to resist our efforts and go their own way.

BE THEIR FRIEND

Being a friend is an important key to effective parenting. Some may question my choice of the word *friend,* pointing out that children have *friends* and need us to be *parents.* This is a good point. Good friends listen to each other, help when they can, but stay on an equal footing without either one taking charge of the other. I agree that the role of a parent is much more than a listener, a friend down the street, or someone you like to be around whom you met at work or school. A friend is not in charge. A parent is.

But we can be much more effective in our role as parents when we have a child's respect. This means a parent can also be a friend, a special kind of friend. This becomes more and more important as the years go by and a child makes more independent decisions. If we don't earn trust and respect, we're not going to sell many of the values we have to offer. So, it's a big advantage for a parent to be a friend as well as someone in charge. And if you are a friend, you have a much better chance of helping a child solve life's problems with values you have to share.

TREAT THEM LIKE CUSTOMERS

How does a good salesman sell cars? It's more than helping a customer pick out a nice car. Unless a customer likes a salesperson, there probably won't be a sale. What if you came in to look at a car and the salesperson scolded you for being late? This happened to me once. Needless to say, I bought a car somewhere else.

You probably wouldn't buy a car from someone who put you down. You'd rather buy a car from someone who seemed helpful and friendly.

The more I've thought about that incident, the more I've realized that being an effective parent is similar to being an effective salesperson. In fact, I've learned more in sales workshops about raising children than I have in classes about being a good father. The principles are the same if you're selling cars or clothes—or rules and values. We have to be good salespeople to get our kids to buy what we want to teach them.

But isn't there a difference between selling a car and selling a value? In the long run it doesn't really matter which car someone buys—but it matters greatly which value someone chooses.

DON'T SEEM LIKE "THE ENEMY"

What's really bad is for a parent to be thought of as an enemy. It isn't too hard to figure out why children might sometimes think of a parent as an enemy. If someone yells at us all the time, we're not going to like it—or the person—very much. Yet most of us yell at our kids. Hopefully, this is offset by all the good things we do for them. And thank goodness children are forgiving. But only up to a point. When we yell at our kids, they then think of us as the bad guy—*the enemy*—at least for a while. It's hard to tell when a youngster has had it with our yelling. Our rating may slip and it may happen rather quickly—especially with an older child or teenager.

It's like a salesperson chewing out a customer. You can't be obnoxious and keep a child's respect. Children need someone who loves them enough to be kind, yet firm and consistent.

BE LOVINGLY FIRM

We need to be firm—lovingly firm. Don't be wishy-washy. Every time you speak to a child, especially when there's trouble, remember that if you don't also come through as a *friend* who really cares, you lose. It's one thing to lose a customer who might have bought a car. But it's quite another to lose a kid. If we want to have any influence in teaching our children, they have to respect us as parents while also feeling that we are friends— not enemies. And this means even when our children irritate us. There's a big difference in how well people follow instructions from someone they like and how well they follow instructions from someone they don't like.

TAKE CHARGE

If you don't quite know how to take charge, you're in good company. Everyone who has felt the burden of responsibility knows exactly how you feel. Taking charge in a family is something like being a quarterback on a football field. Suddenly you have control of the ball and a bunch of big bruisers are headed directly toward you, fully intending to smash you to the ground. Do you run? And if so, do you run to the right, to the left, or straight ahead? Or do you pass the ball way down the field, or hand it off, or throw a little screen pass? You remember the play called in the huddle. So there is a plan—or there was. But now, something's not working. And it's all up to you. The problem is that you have to think and make a decision in a matter of a few seconds.

You've probably had some experience handling an emergency in which you had to make a quick decision. Maybe you've been involved in a car wreck, fire, hurricane, tornado, or earthquake. Maybe you've had to do the Heimlich maneuver when someone was choking. Or maybe you pulled someone out of the water who was drowning. Few people are ever truly prepared to deal with these or most of the other emergencies that come up in life. Risks are often involved. So do you just stand there, or do you take charge and do something?

Whether you're a quarterback with the ball, a mom looking at a choking child, or a person driving down the street when a child runs out in front of your car, one of your toughest jobs in life is to make the best decision you can. You often won't have much time to think. You may have time to ask yourself one question, "What should I do?" Here's an answer that always applies: *Do what's right.*

DON'T BE PUSHY OR A PUSHOVER

No matter how many classes we've taken, how much advice we've heard, or how many books we've read, few parents, if any, are prepared for most of the things that happen.

My wife and I thought raising children was going to be easy. It wasn't. We had a lot to learn. I was really pushy—and lost some big battles that should never have been fought. Other times I was a pushover.

Watching parents react is often as predictable as watching the behavior of two-year-olds. Even when we try to do the best we can, sometimes we just make problems worse. History repeats itself in families like it does in the world.

Children need parents who love them enough to take charge. This is much different from the incorrect notion that *kids rule.* This revolutionary war cry of independence is one of those sayings that spread like a wildfire across the country. But kids don't rule. It's our job to be in charge. We are responsible.

GRIFFIN'S FIRST LAW OF PARENTING

It's a kindness to teach children about obedience and a sense of order from a young age. Sometimes you will need to take a firm stand. But you can be firm and loving at the same time. An example of this is the principle that it's good for children to have the structure of a regular bedtime. But even more important, parents need some quiet time to regroup. *A parent can listen to just so much of high-pitched little voices before becoming impatient and irritable.* This is Griffin's first law of parenting—an observation about us and thousands of other parents.

There comes a time when the deck needs to be cleared of children so parents can rest and do things other than deal with little people. You can pull this off easily. Set a regular bedtime and make it a fun, pleasant time with Mom or Dad. Bedtime for children should not be hurried. This is an important part of the day to give each child your undivided attention.

Bedtime can be a ritual starting with bath time, teeth brushing, and toilet time followed by sitting on the side of the child's bed and talking about the day. Leave plenty of time to listen, read a story, and pray.

When your child is frightened, unplug or turn off the television, and avoid frightening things, especially before bedtime. If he thinks there are snakes under the bed or monsters in the closet, add an extra hug and patiently look under the bed, in the closet, and other places together so that he feels safe. If that isn't enough, a parent can provide lots of comfort by calmly promising, *"I won't let anything happen to you."* Take plenty of time to allay the fears of a spooked youngster. Don't be in a hurry—within reason.

Happy bedtimes with chatting, stories, prayers, and plenty of hugs provide comfort, security, and show how much we really care. Then say good night and the day is over.

But what do you do six minutes later, when a child comes bouncing out of the room asking for a good night drink? Make a good night drink part of the ritual. And my idea of a good night drink is a tiny little drink—maybe a quarter of inch of water in the bottom of a glass—enough to call it a drink, and not too much to fill up a little bladder so that it needs emptying right away.

But after that, what do you do when a toddler comes out wanting another drink or something else she thinks up? Without saying much, just pick her up, give her a hug, and whisk her back to bed. No coaxing. No begging. No arguing. No negotiating. Give her another hug and within seconds have her back in her bed, tucked in, and the door closed. Good night.

And that's it. If a youngster comes out again, and again, and again, like a child who gets in the habit often does, keep putting the child back in bed—quickly. Remember, no coaxing or negotiating. Put the child in bed and expect him or her to stay. When a child repeatedly comes out it's because the youngster has trained the parents instead of the other way around.

So no matter how many times a youngster comes out, put the little person back to bed. He or she may cry a little the first few nights. And that's okay. Show your love by making the going-to-bed ritual a happy time. And as you whisk a youngster off to bed, in a kind, loving voice, say, "I love you." Solving the problem of a child who gets up over and over can make a big difference in providing serenity in a home.

DON'T JUST SIT THERE!

"You mean I'm supposed to be in charge?" you may be wondering a little sarcastically. *"No one around my house seems to know it."*

Well, I still think you're more in charge than the mother who brought her five-year-old to a doctor's office because the child had a large, pigmented mole on her thigh. Before the doctor could even look at the mole, the child went into a rage and kicked him in the ribs. The mom just stood there and let the child violently kick, thrash around, and scream so loudly that two assistants came in to see what was going on.

The child wouldn't let the doctor near her—and the mother didn't do a thing to help. The doctor wasn't even going to take off the mole that day. He was only going to look at it. After forty-five minutes of coaxing and begging, the mother finally convinced the little girl to lift up her dress so that the doctor could see the mole—if he promised to remain across the room.

The child's behavior didn't give the doctor much of a chance to do a careful examination. To make things worse, it looked like a dangerously dark mole that could have been cancerous. Maybe the child was frightened because of a previously unpleasant experience. But that does not excuse the mom from taking charge and controlling the child, who instead controlled the mother, the doctor, the office staff, and the unfortunate people delayed in the waiting room. The mom could have picked up the child and given her a hug while letting her know this behavior was not acceptable.

Even the most effective parent can't control everything a child does. But this mother was in a position to understand the need of the child, who didn't have a clue that the dark patch on her skin could prematurely end her life. Parents often know what is good for a child and what will make a child happy in the long run than the child does at any particular moment. This means that parents must be willing and able to *take charge*.

CONTROL, RESPECT, AND RESPONSIBILITY

It's all about control. Parents want control over their children, and children, having their own minds and wills, want to control themselves. So where does that leave us as parents?

Let's look at it this way. When you fill out medical or school records about your child that ask who the responsible party is, whose name do you write on the form? You are the responsible party for your children. It's as simple as that. Does that mean you have total control over what they do? Of course not. However, while children are in your home, up to a point you, the parents, are responsible.

You and I are responsible. But we don't have control. That's what makes it tough. It would be easier if they were puppets. But they're not. So one of our big jobs is to help children learn to be responsible so that they can make good decisions themselves. Sometimes our children make really good decisions—

---

which is partially because we've been teaching them responsibility already.

RESPECT IS ESSENTIAL

In workshops I often ask parents, "What do your children do that concerns you the most?" The answers often go something like this:

"They tease and provoke each other—and say the other one started it."

"My teenager just disappears."

"They talk back and don't show respect."

"My children don't do what I tell them."

It is frustrating when children don't do what parents expect them to do. This has always been a problem, to some degree.

But what hasn't always been a problem is disrespect. Today, disrespect is rampant in schools from coast to coast. Every teacher I know is concerned. Likewise, parents are appalled by the lack of respect shown to them. This is a serious problem because when children talk back, and get away with it, it's very difficult to teach them the important lessons of life.

We simply can't allow children to grow up being disrespectful. It's completely unacceptable for a child to insult or demean a parent or teacher. A child or teenager who mouths off to a parent, teacher, or other adult in authority must learn that insults, insolence, and profanity will not be tolerated.

If we can't get kids to show us proper respect and to do the little things we ask them to do, how will we get them to accept what we teach them about honesty, drugs, and sex? With this in mind, let's return to the question of how to get kids to do most of the things we want them to do.

Although we can't get kids to do everything we want, we can set high expectations. And we can and must set certain standards of respect. Some things are acceptable and some things are not. Disrespect is absolutely unacceptable. Of course, to gain that respect, we have to show them respect too. And this isn't easy.

BALANCE CONTROL WITH RESPONSIBILITY
Children are not marionettes you can control with strings. Kids just don't work that way. Even if it were possible to make children do everything we want, it wouldn't be good for them—or for us.

"Why?" you may wonder.

Because getting children to do *everything* we want would mean absolute control, which would take away their chance to learn and grow.

"Well, which is it?" you may ask. "How can we set high expectations while giving them all this direction and responsibility too?"

Finding this balance is one of the challenges of being a parent. We can't ever totally control our children. The challenge is to help children become responsible so that they make good decisions.

"But how can I do this? How can I take charge and get respect without pulling the strings?"

It's not easy. In fact, most of us end up being part of the problem instead of part of the solution. Don't think you are the only one who makes foolish mistakes in parenting. You're not. Every parent makes mistakes just like every basketball player throws the ball away once in a while. A player doesn't try to give the ball to the other team, but sometimes the ball gets away, causing a turnover.

One day I was picking up some apples at the grocery store when I heard a mother screaming at her son. Her voice was so loud that everyone around stopped to see what was happening. You might have thought the kid had committed a terrible crime when all he had done was push the cart a little farther ahead of his mom than she thought he should have. So his mother yelled, "Robert—don't move!"

Maybe Robert was pretending he was a parent who was deciding which kind of soda to buy. I don't know. Perhaps his mother was having a bad cash-flow day. Or maybe the kid had tossed a soggy tomato at his brother before they had come to the store. Whatever it was, the mother's yell stopped the boy in his tracks—and humiliated him.

This mom certainly took charge—inappropriately. Obviously, she didn't quite know how to balance her authority with understanding. She didn't use common sense. Most of us find ourselves "in charge" as parents before we know how or what we are supposed to do.

Try talking slowly and softly

Our words and tone of voice make a difference, too. When we sound mean and bossy, it provokes children instead of giving them a reason to want to follow us. And the more upset we get, the easier it is for our voices to grow louder and louder.

When you really want to get attention, try talking slowly and softly. It may sound strange to suggest speaking softly in the midst of contention and anger. But increasing the sound level with yelling seldom works. On the other hand, turning down the volume of your voice often does. It catches children off-guard. The slower and softer you speak, the quieter your child has to be to hear what is said.

You may think if you talk softly that a child won't try to hear what you have to say. Actually, most of the time children will listen to you—especially when you are calm and kind instead of when you act like the Wicked Witch of the West.

This doesn't mean that your child will clean the toilet cheerfully if you ask him in a calm voice, but you can make tasks seem less bad—depending on how you give the instructions.

So what is a good way to ask a kid to clean a toilet? You might try calmly saying, "I can see you're having fun, but would you help me for a few minutes? Here's some stuff that will make this toilet look really clean. It makes a foam when you spray it on. Use some paper towels to wipe it off on the outside and this brush to scrub it on the inside. And that's it."

The youngster probably still won't want to clean the toilet, but this kind of explanation often goes a long way toward getting things done that children need to do.

But just how important is broccoli?

Lots of struggles occur over little things like broccoli. This doesn't mean that we don't want kids to learn to eat broccoli—because that's probably a pretty good idea. But telling a youngster to eat broccoli because it has lots of vitamins and antioxidants doesn't sell much broccoli. We need to find another way.

While some children will do almost anything parents ask—even if they don't want to—with many children, pushy instructions about things like broccoli or picking up toys quickly turn into an argument.

What do you do when a child doesn't want to clean up his room? You probably already know that one good way to teach children of all ages to work is to work side by side with them.

Don't bug 'em!

For a long time, I gave thousands of orders about right things in the wrong way. I didn't get up each morning and say to myself, "I wonder how I can annoy my children today." I just did it.

I became very good at telling our children to do things in ways that bugged them—just as most parents do. Children need and want direction. They need fences—both real ones when they are little so they won't run into a busy street, and *value* fences to protect them from dangerous traps when they are older.

LET THEM PRACTICE MAKING DECISIONS— WITH LIMITS AND GUIDELINES

Children learn by making decisions, so we need to let them practice making decisions about little things—like what to buy when we go grocery shopping.

I know a mother who lets each child who goes shopping with her choose one thing to buy. And we're not talking about toys. Even if you can afford to buy a child a toy every time you go shopping, it wouldn't be a good idea.

Before leaving on a grocery shopping excursion, this mom sits down with whoever is going with her to discuss what the family wants and needs. The mom sets the guidelines. Then when they get to the store, the youngster picks the kind of fruit or vegetable, or maybe a main course or dessert. As a child gets older, he or she may get to plan the entire dinner—and sometimes fix it. Allowing children to make these choices also cuts down on turned-up noses about what's being served. And letting children learn to choose food works so well that some parents let them choose other things they need, like shoes and jeans.

In case you're worried that your kids will choose expensive items, set budget limits. It's good for kids to learn budget constraints—and the difference between wants and needs, which are not the same.

What if a youngster wants a pair of jeans that are over the limit?

Don't get them.

That's the rule.

They can choose, as long as what they choose is within the budget. When kids are older, if they want to spend more than the budgeted amount, they can pay the difference with money they earn themselves. You'd be surprised by how frugal kids can be when they spend their own hard-earned money instead of someone else's.

What if a youngster wants to buy something that looks terrible? You can talk about appropriate clothes. You will probably decide that some things are not going to be paid for with family money. But there's no question that as we let children learn to make decisions about the clothes they buy and wear, there will be some differences of opinion.

What children wear and how they look reflects on us. So when it comes down to what a youngster wears on a particular day, there's the question, "Which is more important—what people think or the opportunity for a youngster to learn to make decisions?"

Does it really matter?
What would you do if one of your children threw a tantrum when you wanted her to wear something nice instead of what she wanted to wear? A good question to ask yourself is, "Does it really matter?"

Sometimes it does. How youngsters dress may affect the way they act. This isn't always the case, but it is often enough to be noticeable. Yet, especially with young children, letting them choose what they wear is a relatively safe way for them to learn to make decisions. But where do we draw the line?

Ask yourself if it will make any difference ten years from now. You might answer that it will if family pictures are being taken. But sometimes a fight about what people wear for a family picture ends up with no picture being taken at all—or some big scowls. These are the day-to-day judgment calls that make parenting tough.

A father with a rigid military background wouldn't allow his teenage son to wear his hair a little longer than the father thought was appropriate. The boy didn't want what most people would consider a far-out hairstyle. He just wanted to express himself by wearing his hair longer than his father's. Over a minor stylistic point, this difference grew into more differences. The boy resented his father profoundly. Ongoing conflicts occurred that were completely unnecessary. Yes, how a youngster looks may affect behavior. But be careful, because the control necessary to accomplish the appearance may come with a price. Making the right calls about such matters takes a great amount of wisdom and good judgment. Think about what you are trying to accomplish. Isn't how a youngster behaves much more important than a hairstyle?

Is it preference or principle?

How can parents decide what's important and what isn't? There is a helpful way to sort this out. Neal A. Maxwell, one of the most profound thinkers and spiritual leaders I know, explained that "some things are a matter of *preference* while others are a matter of *principle.*"

Matters of *principle* are about basic values, while matters of *preference* are about all the other things people can choose that are not as important—like colors of clothes and millions of other day-to-day decisions.

Mixing up *principle* and *preference* is one of the most common mistakes parents make. And yet, even sorting out which are matters of *principle* and which are matters of *preference* may not be simple. But once we figure it out, we can loosen up on *preference* and tighten up a little on *principle.*

Lots of big arguments about unimportant things can set up a pattern of confrontation that may go on and on. Then, instead of being able to talk calmly about matters of *principle,* the youngster may become rebellious.

So how do you get your child to wear appropriate clothing?

You might give a young child a couple of choices, asking, "Which outfit would you rather wear, this one or that one?"

Each morning one mom asked each of her young children what he or she would like to wear that day. This gave her an opportunity to explain about colors that go together and others that don't. The child didn't always get it just right—but these sessions each morning went a long way in helping her children pick up good grooming skills while learning to make decisions.

If it really doesn't matter, let them win

But what do you do when a kid heads out the door without a sweater or jacket when it's chilly outside? When children are young, they need help in knowing how to dress appropriately for the elements. It's just good common sense. And of course you'll want to help youngsters avoid playing in the snow or cold with wet hands or feet. Children often don't understand that very low temperatures can freeze soggy toes or fingers, causing frostbite.

However, many unnecessary battles occur about sweaters and jackets on days when it doesn't make a bit of difference. You may think it strange coming from a pediatrician, but most of the time, it probably doesn't matter much if a youngster gets a little chilly when he chooses not to wear a sweater or jacket.

Kids are more likely to catch colds and other infections from someone with a viral or bacterial infection who breathes germs on them inside at home or in their school classroom than outside playing without a hat or sweater.

Of course, if it's really cold, coats and hats are needed. Use good sense. But remember that school-age kids and teenagers delight in showing their independence by shedding coats and sweaters when it's a little cool. In fact, you've probably noticed that kids often choose to wear shorts to school when you know they can't really be comfortable. And when it's really cold, you'll sometimes see college kids who should know better sitting in the stands at a football game without shirts. So why do they do such dumb things? To show they are tough. It's a peer thing—a demonstration of their independence.

Don't sweat the small stuff

So heading out the door with shorts or without a sweater on a cool day is often a game played by a school kid or teen to challenge a parent's authority. And yes, you have the authority. But all too often the more that's said about the shorts or wearing a sweater, the more the issue is pushed and tested. Richard Calson said, "Don't sweat the small stuff. And it's all small stuff."[2] Well, I agree about not sweating the *small stuff* but I don't agree that it's all *small stuff.* Sorting out the difference is one of the skills we learn as parents. But the sweater issue is one of those things about which I'd usually suggest not invoking your authority. In other words, don't get trapped into making a big deal about wearing a sweater or long pants when it really doesn't matter—which is most of the time. Eventually, youngsters usually figure out it makes sense to be comfortable.

People do stupid things to get attention

Why do you think young people do stupid things?

To be noticed.

So don't notice. Don't set up a needless confrontation. Once parents realize that wearing warm clothing in slightly chilly weather isn't critical to preserving good health, letting kids make decisions about sweaters, hats, and shorts isn't too difficult.

Listen to this wise insight from my friend Hartman Rector, Jr., from his experience raising nine children and leading young people around the world as a navy captain and church leader: "If it really doesn't matter, let them win."

[2] Richard Carlson, Ph.D., *Don't Sweat the Small Stuff . . . and It's All Small Stuff (New York: Hyperion, 1997).*

Although in matters of principle it's important to work out win-win solutions, we don't need to *win* about matters of preference such as flavors of ice cream, colors of socks, and lots of other things that don't really matter.

Life teaches real lessons

On one family's vacation, the plan for the day was to take a hike up a mountain trail in a national park. In spite of protests from her parents, their teenage daughter put on a miniskirt and exaggerated high-heeled shoes. This was definitely not appropriate attire for this activity. No amount of logic changed her mind. Needless to say, she was miserable on the rocky trail. The high heels on the rocks caused several tumbles. By the end of the hike there were scrapes all over her shoes and knees. At that point she didn't need a lecture. Neither did the teenage boy who had an unsuccessful job interview when he showed up in baggy pants and a T-shirt advertising a rock group.

Sometimes life teaches kids lessons better than we can with lectures and pronouncements. And sometimes we should sit back and let life teach its lessons. This is never easy. Sometimes, as we watch our children make choices that we know will have serious consequences, we just cringe. The natural tendency is to rush forward yelling, "Stop!" "Danger!" or "Don't do that!" And sometimes it's appropriate or absolutely mandatory for a parent to intervene—at least to try to stop a terrible mistake from occurring. Other times, no matter how loudly we give our warning, it won't be heard. Certainly we should do what we can when we can—realizing that children, especially older ones, will make their own choices. And sometimes these choices have terrible consequences.

SOMETIMES YOU'LL HIT A BRICK WALL

One family went through a series of particularly terrible experiences with a son who wouldn't listen to their cautions about body-piercing. Against all the advice his parents could give, their rebellious boy had his navel pierced. Although he didn't get hepatitis, tetanus, or HIV from the contaminated needle in the mall jewelry shop, he did get a terrible bacterial infection. Antibiotics were prescribed. No improvement. Another prescription was given. The infection got worse. A series of high-powered shots followed. Still no improvement. By now the spread of the infection was becoming serious. The boy was rushed to the hospital. Cultures showed bacteria that were resistant to all common antibiotics as well as ones kept in reserve for extra-tough infections.

Even after the infection was controlled, more problems occurred. Bacterial endocarditis had damaged two heart valves —another life-threatening problem. This meant open-heart surgery. The valves were replaced. The costs were staggering. The entire family was affected. The boy recovered—but the family was wiped out financially. Plans had to be changed. Everyone sacrificed.

You would think the boy would have learned his lesson after all that. He didn't. Two months later he had his nose pierced.

Sometimes parents run up against a brick wall. Sometimes parents run out of ways to help a youngster who seems aimed at self-destruction. So what do parents do in this kind of situation? The only thing they can do is pray and hope things will change. There sometimes comes a point when parents have to stop spending all of their energy on one child to the detriment of others in the family. This doesn't mean giving up. But sometimes it might mean not *giving* for a while. This sad case made me think of the story of the prodigal son. In spite of everything his family could do, he didn't really learn the reality of all he had been given until he had to go out on his own in the world and learn for himself. Yet even under these most extreme circumstances, loving parents never stop loving, never stop caring, and never give up.

TAKE CHARGE BUT DON'T OVERCONTROL

So take charge as a friend, not as the enemy, being careful not to overcontrol. Then, as youngsters get older, hopefully they will gain the skills to make good decisions about matters of principle.

Along the way, they will sometimes act in self-defeating ways no matter what you do. This is discouraging. But when parents do all they know how to do, youngsters, especially the older ones, are responsible for their own mistakes.

SOMONE NEEDS TO POINT OUT THE MINEFIELDS

It's our job to do everything we can to teach children what's *right* and what's *wrong*. All children need loving parents to teach them the rules of life and to help them figure out how to get along in a world filled with dangers. But it's really tough not to over- or undercontrol.

Every parent who has experienced their teenager learning to drive knows how hard it is to sit in the passenger seat with a new driver at the wheel. Teenagers sometimes think they are indestructible. Many have no fear. Teenage drivers often go along without a clue about the dangers—just as they go through life completely oblivious to its minefields.

A father told me about the time one of his teenage daughters was driving and became distracted by some friends parked on the other side of the road. As she swerved, he yelled for her to watch out because she was about to hit a tree. As the front right tire was going over the curb, she shouted back, "No, I'm not! Don't worry so much!" and jerked the steering wheel so they missed the tree and bounced back onto the road. It was all the dad could do to keep from grabbing the steering wheel.

Being a parent is scary. That is why we need to do everything we can to teach kids to make good decisions from the time they are young. Even then, sometimes we have to grab the wheel or say no. Care enough about your children to be lovingly firm while giving them some room.

* * *

Now, if things are going along pretty well around your place at this very moment, don't get complacent. It probably won't be long before it gets bumpy. And when this happens, you may have good reason to be irritated and angry. You may even be pushed to tears.

This is normal. This is life. This is being a parent.

But you can make things work a little better, starting now. You can decide to be a more effective leader, to take charge—with lots of love.

So stand up and take charge. Don't be afraid to do and say what's right. You've got the authority around your place. Use it. But be wise in how you do it. Be in charge by leading your children like a shepherd leads his sheep instead of driving them like cattle.

In other words, *take charge as a friend—not the enemy.* This is the first of the nine important keys that will make a big difference as you raise your children.

KEYS TO RAISING CHILDREN
1. Take charge as a friend—not the enemy.

2

Make Home
a Happy Place to Be

Don't put that spoon back in the ice cream carton after you've licked it. Think of the germs you just planted in the ice cream."

"Germs?" the youngster repeated.

"Yes, germs. You're supposed to use a clean spoon to dip in the ice cream—not one that's been in your mouth," the child's mom tried to explain patiently. "There are millions of germs in our mouths so when you lick the spoon the germs get on it and then into the ice cream."

This may have been a rather pleasant dialogue—depending on the mom's tone of voice. But what's it like around your place? Kids are always doing irritating things. How do you react? Does your level of yelling get high when you're irritated?

All too often, what we say to our kids is negative—especially when we are worried or concerned about other things. But imagine if you were a kid hearing these things from his parents on a particular day.

Before school:
6:55 A.M. "Get up, or you'll be late for school again!"
7:14 A.M. "But you've got to eat something for breakfast."

7:16 A.M. "You look like something in a grunge video. Put on something decent."

7:18 A.M. "Don't forget to take out the garbage."

7:23 A.M. "Put on your coat. Don't you know it's cold outside? You can't go off to school without a coat in weather like this."

After school:

5:42 P.M. "You forgot the garbage! Thanks to you, we'll have garbage up to our ears for another week."

5:55 P.M. "Come to dinner. Why do I always have to look for you when it's time to eat, when you should have been setting the table?"

6:02 P.M. "How many times do I have to tell you dinner is ready?"

6:12 P.M. "Do you have to come to the table with earphones on your head, plugged into that rotten noise you call music? Can you hear what I'm saying? Take those things out of your ears."

6:16 P.M. "Things are going to have to shape up around here. Your room is a disgrace—and you're going to have to start carrying your load. This isn't a place with servants to wait on you."

6:36 P.M. "Turn off that computer game and unload the dishwasher and put the dirty dishes in it. When we were your age, we had to wash dishes in hot soapy water in the sink."

7:08 P.M. "What are you watching? It doesn't look very good to me—and it's dumb to think you can do homework better with the TV going."

7:32 P.M. "I told you to turn off the TV till your homework is finished. And why are your shoes and candy wrappers in the middle of the floor? I've told you a million times it's easier to put things away immediately than it is to pick them up later. Do you like to hear me yell?"

9:59 P.M. "That stereo is so loud, I can't hear myself think. Go to sleep or you'll be late again tomorrow."

If you were a kid and your parents had said these things to you today, without any positive coaching or cheerleading, how would you feel? And after all this negative input, what would your attitude and performance be like?

TREAT YOUR CHILD AS A GUEST

I know a mom who has a secret weapon—her attitude. She is such a happy, smiling person that she is the key to her particularly happy home. It sounds simple. Be happy. Talk nicely to the people who live with you. "Talk to family members as you would a guest in your home," suggests Jack R. Christiansen.[3] If guests were coming to dinner and they arrived late, you probably wouldn't insult them when they finally got there by saying, "You're forty minutes late, the food's overcooked, and we've been sitting around waiting for you to show up."

And you probably wouldn't point out other things that irritate you about your guests. We usually let a lot go by without comment. Why can't we treat the members of our family as well as we treat our guests? In fact, children really are our guests because, in essence, we've invited them into our homes. Yes, they are a different kind of guest. But looking at the big picture, our homes can be much happier if we think about our children this way.

DEALING WITH AGGRAVATION

Even when home is a happy place to be, there are times that would test anyone's patience. You've probably had your share of

[3] Jack R. Christiansen, *Campus Education Week,* Brigham Young University, August 22, 1997.

days similar to when, in a few unsupervised moments, a toddler and four-year-old had a field day discovering things in cabinets under the kitchen sink. The toddler pulled out and spilled a ten-pound sack of flour, a five-pound bag of sugar, and a green box of dishwasher detergent and then mixed them. Then the four-year-old stirred in some window cleaner and canola oil. The mess on the floor and gooey handprints on the cabinet doors made the finger paints on the wall look like real art.

When the mom found the mess, she suddenly felt very ineffective—as she had many times before. However, instead of yelling, she picked up the children and gave them a squeeze, explaining in a few words that this was not the thing to do—but that she loved them. On the way to the bathtub, little hands and bodies deposited a mixture of oil, sugar, flour, window cleaner, and soap around their mother's neck and in her hair.

THIS MOM GETS AN "A"

Damage control was a major project, but this mother gets an "A" for handling this situation better than she had handled events like this before. Now, the reality is that you and I won't always handle frustrating situations this well. When you do, give yourself an "A." When you don't, see if you can figure out how to handle things better the next time.

Being a happy parent is one of the things that's easier said than done. Most of us try to be happy, but sometimes things just seem to go wrong.

WHAT IRRITATES YOU ABOUT YOUR SPOUSE?

Sometimes you can just sense trouble. The trigger might be a father getting home late from work. The mother had already reached her limit and this finally set her off. After a lousy day at work and things not going all that great around the house, when the kids add more irritation, it's easy for everyone to lose it.

If this has happened to you, don't think you're the only parents that have ever experienced these things. Don't think you're the only ones who become annoyed with each other and the children.

If you think you have a special talent for making annoyances grow into big irritations, grab a pencil and piece of paper. Simply write down the things that irritate you about your spouse.

WRONG QUESTION

No. I changed my mind. Instead of writing down what irritates you about your spouse, write down the things *you* do that irritate your spouse.

"But I'd rather write down the things that my spouse does that irritate me."

Of course you would. But that's not your problem. Your problem is what *you* do to irritate your spouse.

The problem in almost every home is that a husband wants to make his wife a little better and the wife wants to make her husband a lot better. This doesn't work. You can't make the other person be more tidy, more punctual, more considerate, or more anything else. This might seem a little discouraging if you were hoping to get your spouse to do things the way you would like.

But you can do something.

SPOUSE IMPROVEMENT?

My longtime friend Spence Kinard explained something very profound when he said, "Marriages would be more successful if each would try to make his partner happy, rather than good."[4] This is an amazing concept, because most of us spend a lot of time and effort trying to get our partner to do this or that a little better. The reality is that trying to fix up the other person

---

[4] J. Spencer Kinard, *The Spoken Word,* February 9, 1984.

isn't usually very successful. In fact, whether our goal is to get the other one to lose weight, break an annoying habit, or to pick things up around the house, giving instructions to a spouse seldom helps. No one is perfect—no one. And directed spouse improvement just doesn't work.

But there are a couple of steps we each can take to improve things around our home. First, we can focus on making our spouse happy. It's amazing what happens when we stop trying to make a spouse better and concentrate instead on making him or her happy.

That's why I suggested you write down the things that you do that bug your spouse. Think about it. You are the only one who can do anything about the things on your list—and your spouse is the only one who can do anything about the things on your spouse's list.

What if you focused on making your spouse happy—like when you were courting? Don't sit around expecting the other person to make a list and to fix it as a balance. Forget that. Scratch the home-improvement-of-your-spouse list. Just home-improve yourself. In other words, expect lots more from yourself than from your spouse.

LOVE EACH OTHER

Russell M. Nelson, a pioneer in heart surgery, the experienced father of ten children, and a wise church leader, points out something every father should know: "The most important thing a father can do for his children is to love his wife." Obviously children are going to do better when home is a happy place to be. And when we are happy with each other, our home is going to be a much happier place.

START COURTING AGAIN

Even though every parent wants a happy home, all too few work at it to make it happen. The real key is to focus on making your spouse happy. Think about what would happen if you kept courting each other the way you did when you first met. Think of what your home would be like if you treated your spouse like you did when you were first getting to know each other.

"But, I didn't know about . . ." you might be thinking.

Your partner didn't come with a guarantee to be perfect.

So don't worry about trying to make your spouse better. You might have a bargain already. Maybe not. But there's a good chance you do.

GROUCHY PARENTS EQUAL GROUCHY KIDS

Parents who are happy with each other benefit the entire family because grouchy parents mean grouchy kids. Grouchy behavior is more contagious than strep germs. Parents who love each other and who try to have a happy home sometimes have grouchy kids—but parents, for the most part, set the tone.

MAKE YOUR HOME A RETREAT

You can actually make your home a retreat. You can make it a safe house. The world is a rough place. Kids get beaten up in their neighborhoods—if not by gangs, by the kids who should be their friends.

PLAYGROUNDS ARE JUNGLES

It's not much better at school. A playground may be like a jungle. School hallways are often not fun, either. And unfortunately classrooms and some teachers are not only tough, but mean.

There are many great teachers who really care about kids, but every once in a while there's one who yells at the kids all day. Some teachers are so insensitive they make school miserable for the children.

YOU'RE SAFE ONCE YOU CROSS YOUR DRAWBRIDGE

Kids really need a safe place they can come home to. When I was a boy, I imagined our home was a castle—and once I crossed the imaginary drawbridge and got in the front door I felt safe. That's what we've tried to make our home—a safe place where kids could get away from the arrows and spears aimed at them all day at school and in other scary places.

There are some other things we can do to make our homes feel safe, like trying to talk softly and sometimes even having quiet music on—and keeping the noisy television off. It's also nice for kids and parents to get a hug when they come home.

DON'T LET A TROJAN HORSE GET IN

It's not just the cacophony of noise on the television that disturbs a happy home. Even if we get our kids safely inside our home—away from the bullies and drugs and other bad things out there, the television and the Internet can bring bad influences into our homes.[5]

You probably have a pretty good idea of just how many bad programs are on television these days. Besides the terrible movies and sitcoms filled with kids and adults talking about having sex—or doing it—do you know how negative the programming is on MTV and some of the other cable channels?

I read an article about an MTV program in which a gross guy in a run-down warehouse is beating his chest while a frightened young girl waits to be raped. More than a third of kids have watched MTV during a particular week—and typical segments

---

[5] See *www.principles.org,* the *American Family Leauge* Web site, on how to make the Internet safer in your home.

brag about rape, drugs, lesbian sex, and making a mockery of marriage or of being a virgin until marriage.

Realizing the content of this kind of programming makes it even more important for us to set a good example by being very careful about what we watch ourselves and what cable or satellite stations we subscribe to and allow in our homes.

MEDIA INFLUENCES

"What would a Martian think our society was like if he got most of his information from watching our television?" asks television critic and talk show host Michael Medved. A Martian getting his information from watching television soap operas, sitcoms, news, and movies would think that, on Earth, 98 percent of sex occurs between people who are not married to each other, people are preoccupied with sex and violence, most people are divorced, and almost all families are dysfunctional.

The scariest thing Medved said about this is that "our children are little Martians," soaking up all this stuff teaching them that this is normal behavior. Wow! Throw in the fact that in a lifetime a child in our culture spends more time watching television than going to school. Even more alarming is that a person will spend more time watching television than he or she will spend during a lifetime of work!

SITCOMS MODEL DYSFUNCTIONAL FAMILIES

You've probably been alarmed before about the effects of watching sex and violence on television, but as you think about this, I hope you'll be so shocked and motivated that you'll come up with a new plan for markedly limiting television in your home—starting this week. This is important because as bad as society is in real life, it's not nearly as bad as television portrays. Most families are not dysfunctional. Most husbands and wives are not unfaithful. Most marriages do work.

But what about the so-called 50 percent divorce rate we hear about? Michael Medved points out a very significant fact. This is a big lie. Let's look at the real facts. If two people who have not been married before get married today, there is a 75 percent probability that they will stay married. The statistics get skewed when you take the number of marriages and compare them with the number of divorces without considering that many who divorce end up remarrying and then divorce again, sometimes repeatedly.

And think about today's television shows and movies. Very few are about the solid marriages and wholesome families that live in your neighborhood and mine. There are more people doing things right than doing things wrong. But as we watch television, it is easy to become convinced that we are watching the real world. And we are not. We, and our little *Martian* children, are soaking in all this dysfunctional family stuff and believing it.

Yes, we should do what we can to get rid of this junk on television sitcoms and videos. If it seems an uphill battle, it's because many of the writers and producers are more interested in the money than the truth or what's right—and many of them just don't have a clue what a *normal,* happy family is all about.

But there is one thing you and I can do. We can turn the television off—or not turn it on unless there is something on that's wholesome and worthwhile.

REMEMBER BOOKS?

As an alternative to so much television, it really helps to have good books and other reading material around—and to take kids to the library regularly.

A mother was concerned about her children not being good readers. A quick tour through the house provided part of the answer—a television set in each bedroom and not a single book in sight. It's no surprise that the young children and teenagers in this family were not interested in reading.

BOOKSHELVES IN BEDROOMS, INSTEAD OF TVs

Instead of a television in every bedroom, put bookshelves in every room, stocked with books according to a child's reading ability. Some books are exciting enough to read again and again. Janet Lee, a well-known writer and speaker, brought up another idea from her experience of raising seven children: "Some favorite books in our home have become such treasures that our youngsters want to keep them as they get older instead of passing them down to younger siblings. When a book is that good we sometimes get another copy for a younger child."

MAKE BOOKS FUN

Challenge children to read and to use their imagination as they are reading. Ask them to tell you about the characters—what they think they look like, how they think, and what their personalities are like.

Teach a child how to pick good books. If a book doesn't turn out to be interesting, a youngster needs to know it's okay not to finish it and to pick out another one.

MAKE YOUR HOME A GATHERING PLACE

Besides making home a fun place to be with books and games for members of your family, make your home a happy place for young children and teenagers to bring their friends. Yes, it is a bother to have extra people around—especially kids. Every extra body adds to the noise and even good kids disrupt tidiness. But the disadvantages of having extra kids around are of far less consequence than worrying about where young children or teens are and what they are doing when they are not at home. So smile, look happy, and have fun with the friends of your kids. Being a pleasant host for kids isn't really very hard to do. Smile some more. Hand out food. Laugh at yourself instead of them. Compliment them. Encourage them. And act like each one is a very important person. They are.

CHOOSE AND MONITOR THE MOVIES

But what do you do when your kids want to watch questionable movies when their friends come over? Check any movie that anyone brings into your home. Kids may not like this. But try to have your home be a different kind of fun place—where kids want to come to make crazy cookies, do-it-yourself pizzas, or to play games. And some friends may think your rules about television are weird. But that's the way it is—without compromising principles.

Some families literally pull the plug on their television. Others don't have a television in the home at all. As radical as this sounds, it may be better than letting sewage fill our minds. But there are ways to control television so that appropriate entertainment and information can be carefully selected. It takes lots of determination on the part of parents, and working together on the part of kids, to keep the television turned off unless there is something on that's especially good.

But what is acceptable in your home? The kind of movies and television programs you watch will make a strong statement as to what is acceptable. This is another time when what you do says more than what you say. I'm not suggesting that your own entertainment be limited to movies with plots written on a child's level. Many stories that are entertaining and amusing to youngsters are not at all interesting to grown-ups and vice versa. But when parents watch movies that make nonmarried sex and other destructive behaviors seem acceptable, a very low standard is set by default. If a show is garbage for a thirteen-year-old, it's garbage for a sixteen-year-old. And if something's garbage for a teenager, it's garbage for adults too.

Watching inappropriate things on television affects behavior. Even cartoons filled with hitting, fighting, and other violence teach children to solve problems with physical force. The more violence a child sees, the less shocking it becomes. And children copy what they have seen when they play. But it's not just little kids who imitate what they see. People of all ages are influenced by the behavior of characters in movies who teach that it's okay to do the same thing.

Think about why we watch movies. Sometimes we get tired of our usual routine and enjoy escaping into the setting of a movie for a little while. There's more to it than watching a story. While we watch a movie, we usually put ourselves into the role of one of the characters—often one of the leads. For a little while, we vicariously live the life of the character. So if one of our children watches a movie where the characters are involved in violence or sex, they are actually imagining that they are doing it. No wonder movies have such a profound influence. To make it worse, some of the pretend thinking may continue after the movie is over. When you consider the content of a large number of the movies being produced today, this is absolutely frightening.

At one time a *Motion Picture Production Code* helped writers and producers contain some of the destructive power that movies can have. One of its profound guidelines was "The sympathy of the audience shall never be thrown to the side of crime, wrongdoing, evil, or sin." Obviously, that industry guideline is long gone. But this is an excellent guideline for you to use in making choices about movies and videos for your family.

You can find entertaining and decent videos

When you think about the garbage in all-too-many movies and videos being released right now, just the word *video* may make you cringe. But unbelievable as it may seem, there are some excellent videos available that are both entertaining and decent. They are hard to find, but they are available. And since so many new releases contain inappropriate behavior, be very careful in choosing movies that come into your home. One way to find movies that are both entertaining and decent is to check the suggestions and comments on the American Family League's Web site, *www.moviepicks.org.*

Some parents look at the television schedule with their children during Sunday dinner, while they go over schedules for school activities, games, practices, and other things. When there's something really good coming up they plan to watch it together. And when there isn't, the TV isn't on unless they decide to rent a good movie.

WHAT ARE THEY LEARNING?

It makes lots of sense not to invite destructive influences into our homes. Sometimes they get in anyway. Even when we're watching something that seems decent, inappropriate things can slip in. When they do, take advantage of these opportunities as teaching moments—asking the kids what they think of the situation they have just seen. Whether it's disrespectful behavior, grotesque events, living together without marriage, a dysfunctional family, or news like the 1998 White House scandals, flip off the television without making a big fuss and talk. But won't the kids protest? Maybe. But play it cool and stick to your standards.

Kids may moan and groan if you punch the remote when the story makes it seem okay to be disrespectful, play around with sex, or do other inappropriate things. But that's okay. What kids see in sitcoms and movies teaches them what to expect in life. After watching some of these programs, it's no surprise that kids today show so little respect for their parents and teachers. It's no surprise that we have so much violence. And it's no surprise that there are so many teen pregnancies and sexually transmitted diseases. Hour after hour, day after day, kids are taught step-by-step through television how to live without rules, values, or real happiness.

"But if you don't let kids watch these things, how will they know how to handle them when they get out in the world?" someone asked. Good question. Kids learn from the experiences of others—both positive and negative. But what are they learning? Suppose grotesque violence is put in a movie to glorify brutality? Sensitivities are lowered—and what once may have seemed shocking isn't as shocking anymore. The more one sees of this kind of film, the more acceptable violence becomes. These films certainly do not teach anything about how to cope with problems in the real world or how to live happy and productive lives.

The same thing is true in watching sitcoms that include more and more jokes about sex and nonmarried sexual behavior. These all too soon become the norm. Consequences are laughed away—or are accepted as part of the game. Or what about watching movies in which the good-looking leading characters have fun with sex without thinking about marriage or possible consequences? Think about the most popular movies around today. How often is there sex without marriage? Sometimes it's on-screen and sometimes it's just implied. On-screen sex is never acceptable. But there's also a big problem in watching stories that make it seem just fine to have nonmarried sex. It isn't. But you certainly don't learn this from watching most new movies today. In the real world, behaviors have consequences. Good movies entertain without encouraging negative behavior. Really good movies entertain while promoting good character. And there are hundreds of good movies and videos that are entertaining and decent. But when you get one that isn't, it's worth a click—and the time to talk.

How you handle the television remote in your home is a major parenting decision. Significant principles are involved. But it goes beyond deciding what you want to do. To succeed in monitoring what comes into our homes takes lots of love, teaching, input, and the involvement of young children and teenagers. Even though it's difficult, some families do a pretty decent job of limiting trashy sitcoms and videos.

Some may think that if you don't allow your children to watch crummy movies or programs on television, they will go somewhere else to see them. And this may happen at times. But you probably have more influence on your youngsters than you think, especially if you really work at being close to them. And you can talk with the parents of your children's friends along the way—and some of them may raise their standards to meet yours.

IT'S A "FAMILY RULE"

You've probably heard about win-win negotiating. This principle is as important in a family as it is in business. Listen so that you know the other person well enough to explain his position—and then try to come up with an answer that works for both of you. So how do you come up with a win-win deal if kids want to watch a movie filled with sex or violence that you don't want them to see? The win-win answer may be to take a movie back to the video shop and rent a different one that doesn't contradict family values. Obviously, sometimes this won't work. It certainly isn't a snap. It can help to have principles that your family follows. And it often helps to say, *"It's a family rule."*

Family rules can provide the kind of authority and standards in a family that the Constitution has the basis of law in our country. It helps children to grow up learning that *family rules* are unchangeable and apply to everyone in a home. When you're trying to maintain an important principle, citing a *family rule* is usually more effective than throwing out an order that a youngster thinks you've cooked up personally for him.

We can be much more effective when we don't put ourselves on one side and our children on the other. It's important for kids to understand that we are on the same side.

Loosen up and be a nice ogre

If kids take a stand that's on the other side of your family rules, be pleasant and smile a lot. Don't sound like an enemy general demanding unconditional surrender. Loosen up. Sometimes you can even add a little humor—about yourself, never putting down your child.

Add a light touch to being firm

When a kid doesn't quite get it—and yells "Why?" it may be tempting to yell back, "Because I'm the mom" or " 'Cause I'm the dad." Although being the parent is sufficient reason for a child to be obedient, and once in a while may be the right thing to say, telling children to do something because you're the mom or dad can be very irritating to them.

Instead of annoying his children by exercising his authority, one father lightens things up when he says: "I know you think I'm so ancient that I'm almost extinct, but I *am* the dad around here." This sounds much better than yelling, "I'm the dad and you're the kid." Keep things light as you stick to principles. You'll seem more human. A better way to take a firm stand is to gently say: "I love you too much to let you get away with that."

In other words, when you're taking a tough stand, like you have to do sometimes, be a *nice ogre* instead of a mean one. You can turn tense moments into light ones. It isn't always easy. And be careful not to tease or demean anyone else. Instead, when you focus a joke on yourself, it's more likely to get your point across than if you make light of someone else. Joking around with kids and their friends will make you seem like a friend, which will help take the edge off some of the firm positions you'll need to take. And when kids have fun at your place they are more likely to hang out there instead of somewhere else. The longer you're a parent, the more you'll realize why this is so important—even though it may seem like you are feeding a platoon of marines!

LOVE, HUGS, AND YOUR OWN TRADITIONS

If you visited the home of a family I know, you would notice a little brass plate on the inside of the door engraved with three words: "Return with honor!" What a powerful reminder. Every time the children, or the parents, go out the door, they see their mom's reminder—"Return with honor."

Another nice tradition is to give a little hug and say "I love you" whenever someone in the family leaves the house or comes home.

You'll create your own traditions—but whatever you do, do what you can to make your home a happy place and a retreat from the rough world outside.

One day, a four-year-old brought his mother a picture he had drawn and said, "I love you, Mommy." The mom gave him a big hug and they sat there on the step for a long time. He suddenly looked concerned and asked his mom if she had seen the bears in their backyard. With a big smile, she reassured him that there were no bears anywhere nearby. This satisfied him but then he wanted her to read him the storybook about the biggest bear, which she did.

The four-year-old soaked up love from his mom, who sensed this was the most important thing she could do right then— more important than cleaning out the refrigerator, more important than the book she wanted to finish, more important than collecting for the cancer drive, and more important than anything else right then. This is about as good as it gets.

Being a parent is the most important job we'll ever have. And it really helps to have home be a happy place.

KEYS TO RAISING CHILDREN
1. **Take charge as a friend—not the enemy.**
2. **Make home a happy place to be.**

3

Give Your Children Something Priceless— Your Time

I t's fun to give a child a bike, puppy, new outfit, computer, or some other material thing we can buy. But time is a better gift than material things. In fact, the most valuable thing we can give a youngster is our time.

One day, a four-year-old came running into the kitchen and asked his mom to take him to the park to see the ducks. The mom explained that she couldn't drop everything right then. The little boy obviously felt disappointed but seemed satisfied when his mother promised they would go see the ducks the following morning.

After breakfast the next day when the mother started getting the children ready to go to the park, the four-year-old started crying. Since they were on their way to do what he wanted, his mom asked why he was so sad. The little boy sobbed as he answered, *"You were going to take me to the park all by myself. You promised."*

SPEND TIME ALONE WITH A CHILD
We often forget how much it means to a youngster to have special time alone with us. Of course, you can have lots of family

fun together—but there's nothing quite like a child having a mother or father completely to himself.

But couldn't he have had just as much fun if another child went to the park too? Well, would you rather have your own appointment with the governor or would you like to share the time with someone else? You'd probably rather have your own appointment—just as your child would usually rather have solo time with you than share you with someone else.

I know a mom who has a tradition of spending a whole day with each of her children. They call it their *day with Mom.* Sometimes they go on walks or bike rides. Sometimes they take a picnic lunch and sometimes they just get a pizza. Other times they go shopping or to a museum. When I asked, "How do you find the time?" she answered, "It means juggling other things I have to do, but it's worth it."

THE BEST PART OF A
SECOND GRADER'S VACATION

One summer, our whole family went on a once-in-a-lifetime trip to Europe. This was a family adventure to end all adventures. We saw chateaux in France, canals in Amsterdam, Big Ben and a royal horse show in England, and the beauty of Ireland.

When the summer was over, the second graders in my son's class were asked to draw a picture and tell the class about the best part of their vacation. What do you suppose our son picked as the highlight of his summer?

Not airplanes—or foreign capitols.

These weren't even close. His picture had nothing to do with Europe or jet planes. Our second grader drew a picture of a lake and a mountain. The greatest adventure of the summer to him was a spur-of-the-moment outing with his dad.

"What was so great about that little trip?" you might wonder. Not much. After work one afternoon, we threw a couple of sleeping bags in the car along with a tent, fishing poles, and I shouldn't forget to mention the bargain inflatable raft that turned out not to be such a bargain.

My wife rounded up the camp cooking stuff—and some food, knowing we wouldn't catch any fish. When we arrived at the lake, we unloaded the car, pumped up the raft, and soon were on the lake tossing out our fishing lines. Our seven-year-old thought he had a bite, which turned out to be a snag.

Then all of a sudden things got exciting—and I was sitting in cold water. One of the plugs in the raft had worked itself loose, explaining why it was such a bargain. After pushing the plug back in and paddling to shore, we dried our clothes over the fire, cooked dinner, climbed into our sleeping bags, and talked awhile before falling asleep.

In the morning we got up early, cooked breakfast, paddled out on the lake for a few minutes, loaded the car, and drove home. I was a little late to work.

That little excursion may not sound like much fun to you. But it was to a seven-year-old boy. To him, that little trip was more important than flying to Europe. On the big trip, he was one of six kids. On the little trip to the lake, he had his dad to himself.

TEACHING MOMENTS

On the way to a hockey game with her father, an eleven-year-old looked up at her dad and asked if she could pose some questions about getting married. What a teaching moment. The dad pulled the car over and they talked. A few minutes later, tears of happiness were streaming down the young girl's face as she told her father that he could always trust her.

The father doesn't remember who won that hockey game or even who played, but he remembers some very important questions were asked and answered that evening.

Take a kid on business trips

A parent can build a lasting relationship by spending time alone with a youngster more than in any other way. One father frequently took his son with him on business trips. While driving, they talked about all sorts of things—war, death, income taxes, work, baseball, honesty, life, and sex.

He set up teaching moments to talk about important things while they had fun. As they drove along on those trips, they read articles from *Reader's Digest,* guessed how far it was to landmarks ahead, played word games, drilled times tables, and came up with ideas for things that hadn't been invented yet. They also talked about history, geography, and what was going on in the world. It was like the son having his own private tutor—only he didn't know he was being tutored.

On those trips the father and son often thought of ways to do things easier, faster, or better. The time the father gave his son was more important than if he had put money in the bank. And the boy grew up wanting to please his father. After all, how could a boy disappoint someone who took him on trips and taught him interesting things?

Start when they are little

When this boy grew up, he took each of his children with him on errands and excursions. When the children were babies and toddlers, the one-on-one outings with their dad were short. As time went on the activities grew longer. This took a big load off the mom and the children loved it.

Kids never forget

Whether the excursion is taking a youngster when a parent has to go back to work for a while, spending a half-hour at the playground, taking a little hike, camping in the rain, coaching softball or Little League, cooking out, building a tree house, squeezing in a quick trip to a museum, or going kayaking, these times are worth every minute.

Kids don't forget excursions like these with their dad or mom. They know you care enough to be crazy and their friend.

It wasn't always easy for me to be fun with our kids. Even though I took them to a lot of places, they thought I was *weird*, meaning I was far too serious. The kids were always telling me, "Loosen up, Dad," which was good advice, because the people you enjoy being around smile and are happy. When you are having fun with a youngster, barriers fall and a child can discover you are a friend instead of an enemy.

HOW DO YOU MAKE IT COME OUT EVEN?

When I suggest taking one child at a time on excursions, someone who has more than one child often asks, "Won't the other kids think it isn't fair?"

This may happen at first. But as soon as a child catches on that you're going to spend some time all alone with him or her, you won't be hearing that "it isn't fair" very often—especially if you always have a one-on-one event for each youngster coming up and marked on the family calendar.

But how do you make it come out even? It never will come out exactly even. But when kids know something is coming up for them, they are almost always satisfied.

And once you get started, kids look forward to these times with their mom or dad so much that if there's not one of these days on the calendar, children will often keep asking until an event is scheduled.

A tradition of early breakfasts

Lois Jensen, an elementary school teacher and the mother of seven, created a tradition of having breakfast with one of her children before anyone else was up.

"How did you get a kid to wake up early to do something with you?" I asked.

"At first it took some doing," she answered. "But it was so

much fun to sit on the porch while we sipped hot chocolate or read stories in a tree house, that all I had to do was mention breakfast with Mom and the kid got up."

I don't imagine she got up in the tree house with her youngsters very often, but the times she did built lasting memories.

When I asked her what other activities she did on those early mornings before work, she answered, "Sometimes we read a story or poems together. Sometimes we munched on fresh fruit or fixed something special for breakfast. Other times we went on an early morning nature walk."

Being particularly interested in how a working mom was able to do lots of one-on-one things with her children, I asked her how she did it.

"I'm not going to tell you it was easy," she answered, "because it wasn't. I tried to arrange my work schedule so I could be home as near to when the children got home from school as possible."

She also explained that she tried to take a youngster, one at a time when possible, with her when she needed to go somewhere. "Whenever one of us needed to go somewhere, I thought it might as well serve more than one purpose—and often turned an otherwise dull errand into something fun."

Just think what kids can learn by going with you to a bookstore, fabric shop, post office, fish market, bank, or even the garbage dump.

MOMS WHO WORK

If you happen to be a mom who works, you may wonder how in the world you can make time to do things with your children. I know it isn't easy. Whenever I get upset about not having enough time, I try to remember that everyone has twenty-four hours to spend in each day. No one gets any more time than anyone else. You never have enough time—but you take it. You've got evenings and weekends.

A working mom put it this way: "When I come home from work I'm really tired. And sometimes the children really get to me. I try, and I think I'm a pretty good mom."

Now this mom really was a very good parent—and my guess is that you are, too. There won't ever be enough time. Whether the time you give children is stopping in the middle of what you are doing to give a hug, answer a question, or just listen, you're saying that you care and they are important to you.

Now go for it. The time you spend with kids will be more valuable than almost anything else you can give them.

HOW CAN A SINGLE PARENT SPEND ONE-ON-ONE TIME WITH A KID?

How does a single parent spend one-on-one time with a child? "I'd love to go places and do things with each of my children alone, but as a single parent, who would take care of my other kids while I spend time with just one?" a mom asked me at a workshop.

This is a tough one. You can focus time on one youngster for moments or minutes at home, or wherever you are. Tuning out the others isn't easy—but I know some single moms who are really good at it. Besides this, it's important to get away with each child alone. This isn't easy. But a single parent can trade off with another single parent to take care of her children while she goes shopping, runs errands, goes out with a friend, or takes one of her children alone with her on a little outing.

And don't forget getting some help from grandparents—or the non-custodial parent.

TIME IS THE BEST GIFT

Time is the most valuable gift we can give our kids—or anyone. Money and things are soon gone. But memories and feelings of love can last a lifetime.

Care about kids enough to spend time with them. Wherever

you go will be special to them—if they are with you and you are having fun together. Children and teenagers need parents who will listen and visit with them a little every day—not just on *special events*.

BUT I DON'T HAVE ENOUGH TIME

This may all sound good, but you're probably thinking that activities like these take too much time—time you don't have and don't know where you'll find, especially while you're struggling to keep up with all you have to do at work and at home.

I understand this. I didn't know either. But I hope you're smart enough to find the time earlier than I did—because a couple of our kids needed more time with me than I gave them. Children need parents who take time to play with them, which doesn't happen enough in today's busy world.

WHAT CAN YOU TALK ABOUT WITH A KID?

Once you get in a one-on-one situation with a youngster, either at home or on a little getaway excursion, what do you say to them? Many people, especially dads, find it hard to think of anything to talk about with little children. How do you get started?

Just talk. Talk about what you see in the yard or wherever you are—worms, butterflies, trash in the street, what roads are made of, favorite foods, desserts, and even silly things. Once children are comfortable talking with you about little things, they are more willing to talk about more important things. Of course, anything a child wants to talk about is important.

"Boring" and "Nothing"

When you ask a youngster, "How was school today?" expect the answer to be: "Boring." This is typical. Don't be annoyed. This is how they tick. So when you or anyone else asks a kid, "What did you do in school today?" the answer is almost always: "Nothing."

If you persist, asking, "Come on now, you must have done something. What did you do?" the answer is usually, "The same old thing."

Most kids give these answers. It's like they all read from the same script. So if this happens to you, don't be surprised. You're just getting the programmed voice-mail response that comes from kids' brains.

There are a couple of ways to get past this automatic programming. Instead of asking questions with one-word answers, such as "What did you do at school today?" try saying something like, "Teach me something you learned in history today." Or you might say, "See if you can stump me with one of your spelling words." Another question that kids will usually answer is, "What are the worst things going on in your life right now?"

You may be surprised at the replies. A kid may tell you about the mean things friends have done—or once in a while a child may tell you about a conflict with a teacher that you otherwise would never have known about.

You could also ask, "What's the best thing that's happened to you this week?"

Or you might suggest, "Let's make a list of fun things we might be able to do together."

If you get some answers that are within reach, like going to the mall or, better still, the library or planetarium, you've got some good ideas of what you can do together.

PART OF THE ADVENTURE IS GETTING THERE

And wherever you go, part of the adventure is getting there—on the metro, train, bus, or even by walking.

One afternoon we drove to a town fifty miles away, caught a Greyhound bus to another town, where we boarded an Amtrak train back to the town where our car was waiting for us to drive home. We didn't get home until two in the morning, but this little excursion was remembered for a long time. Can you imagine what that boy told his friends about his adventure with his dad?

Figuring out how to schedule this excursion was much easier than you may think. Once the idea popped into my mind, it only took a few minutes on the phone to check on bus and train schedules and to figure out how it would work.

When a dad realized his son needed some of his time, he got out some frequent flyer tickets and invited a happy little boy to go on an overnight adventure. They crammed clothes into overnight bags, hurried to the airport, missed a flight, and then caught the next one. They had one adventure after another, beginning with the curious kid getting lost on the wrong side of airport security.

But the boy was the boss for the day. Besides going to the beach, they went to an amusement park. They didn't do much talking, but they certainly communicated. Flying home after an exciting day, more than memories had been built.

FUN ISN'T ALWAYS EXPENSIVE

Fun times with kids don't have to cost a lot of money. As we learned when our seven-year-old chose the little trip to the lake over the expensive trip to Europe as the highlight of the summer, the things that cost the least can mean the most. And in case you think this is just an isolated example, it isn't. Returning to school after a spring break, the students were asked to make a top-ten list of the favorite things they did. "A ride with my grandpa in his truck," was number one on the list of an eight-year-old—far ahead of several other seemingly more exciting, and expensive, family activities. Most people don't have any idea how much a child values personal time with a parent or grandparent.

Whether it's a forty-six-minute ride in a pickup truck, going for a swim, playing checkers, or a foosball or table-tennis tournament, the time a child spends alone with a parent or grand-parent builds relationships and is remembered for a lifetime.

After talking about games and fun, you might get the idea that I think life is a never-ending summer camp. I don't—not at all.

Work projects can be fun, too

We do many work projects around our home. And we encouraged our children to figure out ways to earn money at our home, our office, or in the neighborhood. I know a teenage boy who started a window-washing business. Although he did this mostly on his own, his dad was a helpful source of support—coaching him about creating a business plan and a billing system.

Something magic happened one night when I was crawling around on my hands and knees in a tight crawl space with three of my grandsons. Their dad had just converted a storeroom into a study room, where they planned to keep the family computer. Since the storeroom didn't have a telephone outlet, they needed a new phone line for the computer's modem. The project looked simple. We could run a new phone line from the outside phone box, through a hole drilled from the outside of the house, into the crawl space. Then we could pull the wire around footings and partitions and up through a new hole in the floor, close to where the computer would be in the new room.

At first, climbing down through the trapdoor in the closet floor into the dirty crawl space wasn't the most fun thing I could think of doing. But looking up at the wide eyes of an eight-year-old boy standing in the closet, I asked my grandson if he had ever been under his house. The answer was no, but it was quickly obvious that exploring in a dark crawl space would be an adventure for an eight-year-old. "Ask your mother if you can bring me a flashlight and then stay down here to help me," I suggested.

Permission was reluctantly granted and soon we were stretching a measuring tape to see how much phone cable we needed to buy. The noise soon attracted two more grandsons, each of whom eagerly accepted assignments to hold flashlights and plot the best course for the wire. Instead of drilling through concrete, we decided it would be easier to bring the wire through a drier vent flashing. But it had been smashed—maybe by a lawn mower. No problem.

At the building supply store we bought the needed fifty feet of wire, an eighteen-inch drill bit, grommets, a new drier vent assembly, and a big roll of duct tape. By the time we got home, it was way past the boys' bedtime. Their mom wanted to call a halt to the project for her boys, but I protested, explaining their assistance was essential to accomplishing this important work.

Soon the three young workers were back under the house, each at his assigned position. Of course there were trips up into the house to tap while others listened to be sure the hole wouldn't be drilled into existing electrical wires or heating ducts. After everyone agreed as to where the hole should be, I drilled the hole and eager young fingers pushed the cable from the crawl space, through the new hole, and up into the room.

Changing the drier duct assembly was not as easy. Finally, the old one was removed and the new one pushed into place— well, almost into place. Connecting the new assembly to the existing duct took many pieces of duct tape—put on by so many fingers and hands that frequent stopping and starting was necessary to connect the duct flashing assembly to the duct— which wasn't a very good fit.

But the duct assembly wasn't the only thing that wasn't quite long enough. The fifty feet of new phone cable didn't quite reach around the casing of an outside door. A slight miscalculation. Maybe if we had drilled holes in each floor joist along the route, we could have saved enough wire to make it. Not so. While contemplating options, three young boys and a tired grandpa lay on their backs in the darkened crawl space under the house. The squeaky voice of the eight-year-old broke the middle-of-the-night silence with an interesting question: "Granddad, is this the most fun you've ever had in your life?"

While I was trying to think how to answer the question behind this profound statement, my young grandson went on, "This is the most fun I've ever had in my life."

Think about what had happened crawling around under the house that night. We were not on a ten-thousand-dollar safari. We were not water-skiing on a beautiful lake. We were not sitting in expensive box seats at a football game. We were not at the mall buying toys. Instead, we had been crawling around in the dirt under a house late at night, figuring out where to run a telephone cable, pulling and pushing wires, and duct-taping a drier vent assembly. To my grandson, doing this with me was the most fun he had ever had in the eight years of his life. This work project had meant more to him and was more fun than hitting triples and home runs in his Little League baseball games—or being the winner of his school's pass, punt, and kick football contest. Spending time with his grandpa that night had been more fun than all the great family vacations and other events he could remember. If you ever wonder about the value of spending time with a kid—doing rather ordinary things— think about the words "Grandad, this is the most fun I've ever had in my life!"

SIT DOWN TO LISTEN—A GOOD IDEA FOR DOCTORS AND PARENTS

Sitting down to listen and talk is really important. I learned this while a colleague and I conducted time-motion studies in medical offices and clinics. If you know doctors who dash into the examination room, stand there for a couple of minutes, and then vanish, this is unfortunate. When this happens, you can sense they are in a hurry—and it makes you feel like they aren't very interested in you.

When I'm the patient, I don't like it when the doctor pops into the room for only a few moments. On the other hand, we studied the occasional doctor who came into a hospital or office exam room, sat down, casually listened, checked what he needed to, and visited without hurrying—even though we knew he was very busy. He made each of his individual patients feel important.

Hopefully, what I learned in that study helped me to be a better doctor in the years that followed. I certainly tried. Whenever I made hospital rounds or saw patients in my office, instead of standing there waiting to hurry off I always sat down—and listened. And patients seemed to like the fact that I was interested in them.

The same thing applies to putting little kids to bed or listening to teenagers. Take time to care. The amazing thing is that it doesn't take very much extra time. And the extra time it takes not to act like you're hurried with your children is well worth it.

Bedtime visits with kids

A good quiet time to spend with children is bedtime. Make it special, so each child knows that he or she will have time with you alone—at least for a few minutes. Sitting on the edge of the bed lets a young child, or teenager, feel special.

"My mom used to come in my room and sit on the bed and we just talked," a young mother told me. "This didn't just happen once in a while. It was part of growing up."

"Although I didn't admit it, I really liked my mom coming in to talk with me," a young friend told me.

At these times, a boy doesn't have to be cool or worry about what his peers will think. Sometimes kids will really open up during these late night talks.

READ TO KIDS OF ALL AGES

Children love to hear stories, either from books or those you make up on the spot. Reading good books to a child is one of the best ways you can spend time together. You can learn about life. You can learn about people. You can explore the world together. Of course, I'm talking about reading to children of all ages—little ones who can't yet read, older kids, and teenagers. By reading to preschoolers, besides teaching them to love books you will teach them things they will remember all their lives.

MAKE UP YOUR OWN STORIES

Children also love to hear made-up stories about imaginary kids that match their age and situation. Telling stories about imaginary children we called Betty and Susan was a great way to teach our girls things we wanted them to learn.

Now our children have their own kids, and they tell them some of these Betty and Susan stories as well as new ones that fit their children's particular needs and situations.

Evan A. Schmutz, a busy attorney and father of four, has taken this storytelling a step further. Some of Evan's stories are about mythical princes and princesses who have all sorts of adventures. The stories always teach something about loyalty, integrity, or another important value he wants to teach his children. The stories have become so popular they have been told and retold over the years with added extensions to the tales along the way.

Children also like to hear stories about us—if we're careful not to make our own experiences unreachable.

SOMETHING MAGIC MAY HAPPEN

Businesspeople take clients out to play golf, eat dinner, or watch a ball game. The idea is unrushed time to talk. Time we spend doing similar things with our kids may be more valuable than taking out a business client. Just as on business outings, nothing very meaningful may happen with a youngster on a particular event. But like our impromptu camp-out, when the plug popped out of the raft, something magic sometimes happens.

When a father took his young son to a baseball game and the pitcher was thrown out and fined for losing his temper, there couldn't have been a better teaching moment. The lessons about choices and consequences in sports are so much like life that sporting events set up many opportunities to teach.

SOME EVENTS WITH KIDS WILL BE BOMBS

Don't expect every event with your kids to be a smashing success. Some will be bombs.

And if you're thinking that these one-on-one outings sound good, but wonder if we ever went anywhere as a family, the answer is yes. But don't ever take six kids to an opera! We learned this valuable lesson by doing it once. This is a much better one-on-one youngster event.

Taking two grade-school kids to a ball game may be lots of fun. But taking more than one child turns into more of a social outing for them than a time for interaction between a parent and a child.

Imagine two kids in the backseat of a car, or on a subway, on the way to a basketball game. The kids will laugh, giggle, and poke each other while bantering back and forth about *kid* things. This is okay, and there are times when this is exactly what you want them to do. But when you take two kids in this kind of setting, you are the chauffeur or tour guide. Very little communicating occurs between a parent and either of the children, unless you're fussing at them to be more quiet or to quit kicking the back of your seat.

One way to make an activity work with more than one youngster is for the parent to enter into the fun. It isn't always easy to step out of your role as a grown-up, but when you do it lets kids know you are human. But this is an entirely different objective than a one-parent one-child event.

Also, when you take more than one youngster to things that cost money, the costs multiply. As young parents, we occasionally got tickets for the whole family for ice shows, ball games, musicals, stage plays, circuses, rodeos, and other events. This is nice sometimes, but we soon learned this was expensive and usually not as beneficial as one-on-one activities.

KIDS NEED A PARENT—NOT A GOVERNOR

It's important to spend much more time with each youngster every day than the national average time most fathers spend talking or doing something with a youngster. Too often this is moments instead of meaningful minutes or hours. Unfortunately, the average individual time most mothers spend with a youngster each day isn't enough either.

Friendship between a parent and a child is something like love between a husband and a wife—both need constant nurturing. So a few minutes here and a few hours there are really important.

If you're still worried about the time it takes to be a parent, I know what you're talking about. There isn't enough time in a day to get everything done that we need to.

Work certainly took too much of my time. If I could do it again, I'd get home from work much earlier every day—well, almost every day. I'd be home for dinner. I'd be there more when the children needed me. I don't know any parent with grown kids who has said "I wish I'd spent more time at work." Talking about his young children, Governor David Beasley explained, "They don't need a governor, they need a dad."[6]

[6] Governor David Beasley of South Carolina speaking in Washington, August 2, 1997.

We can learn a lot from this. My kids had a doctor for a dad—and even though I stitched up lots of their cuts, put casts on their broken arms, and took care of many of their other medical needs, I was gone far too much of the time doing these things for others when I should have been home with them. Our kids may have needed me as their doctor once in a while—but they really needed me *as their dad* lots more of the time than I was available to them.

Ask any father with grown kids what he would do differently if he could go back in time. One of the answers will almost always be "I wish I'd spent more time with my family." So do it—starting today. Give your children something priceless—your time.

THINGS TO DO WITH A YOUNGSTER

> Learn a computer program
> Invent something
> Explore a historical site
> Go to a ball game
> Wallpaper a room
> Play catch
> Cut wood
> Plant a garden
> Work on cub or scout advancements
> Go on a photo shoot
> Check homework
> Go on a daddy-daughter date
> Go to a hockey game
> Take a youngster when you have to go back to work for a while
> Spend a half-hour at the playground
> Take a little hike
> Go camping, even if it's raining
> Be a Little League coach or a softball coach

Have a cookout
Build a tree house
Take a quick trip to a museum
Go kayaking
Go fishing
Sit down and tell one or two of your famous stories
Go for a walk in the morning
Go running
Go to a bookstore
Take a load of garbage to the dump
Go to a repair shop
Go to the post office
Visit a tire factory
Tour a soda pop bottling plant
Go shopping at the mall
Choose paint colors for a project
Go to an art gallery
Attend a fashion show
Go to a symphony
Attend a little theater production
Bake bread
Go to a fish market
Visit a bus station
Go to the bank
Play checkers or chess
Work on a craft project
Make gifts
Make a cake
Visit a nursing home and take a gift
Iron clothes and sew on buttons
Head to the woods, a lake, or the mountains
Go to the library
Visit a planetarium
Visit a university

Tour a box factory

Go on an adventure in the city

Spend an afternoon riding the metro

Go for a short train ride

Plan a little bus trip

Visit places that might lead to an interesting career

Go for a ferry ride

Plan an ongoing table tennis tournament

Set up a window-washing business

Visit a television studio

Tour a newspaper office

Tour a printing plant

Grow and sell tomatoes

Make up some adventure stories

Visit a sawmill

Play tennis

Tour an auto assembly plant

Write a book about ostriches

Tell stories about their grandparents and great grand-parents

Tell stories about when you were a kid

Play golf

Go to an opera

Go to a musical

Go to a carnival

Plan an adventure at a circus

Visit a fabric shop and get some patterns and material

Make cookies

Learn to cook in a Dutch oven and make a special family dinner

Plant some seeds in indoor pots

Set up an investment account

Go to a city council meeting

Attend a legislative session
Visit the state capitol

KEYS TO RAISING CHILDREN

1. **Take charge as a friend—not the enemy.**
2. **Make home a happy place to be.**
3. **Give your children something priceless— your time.**

4

Don't Say Much Until You Listen

One day I sent my teenage son on an important errand in my car, explaining that I needed something immediately. The errand should have taken twenty minutes— twenty-five at the most.

Thirty minutes passed. He hadn't returned.

Sixty minutes came and went. No son.

I was getting upset. After an hour and twenty minutes, he still wasn't home. To make things worse, I was sick and was burning up with a fever, and my head was spinning. Still, I kept telling myself, "Don't yell when he gets home."

As time passed I became even more angry. Finally, two and a half hours after leaving on a twenty-minute errand, my son walked in and started to speak. "Dad . . ."

Without taking time to listen, I interrupted, imposing a sentence without a trial—or hearing. "Give me the keys."

My son tossed me the keys, knowing it meant he wouldn't be driving for a while. When I demanded to know where he had been, my son didn't say a word—he just glared at me.

"I asked you a simple question. Where have you been?" I asked.

Silence.

"I'm your father and I want to know what you've been doing for the past two and a half hours when I sent you on a twenty-minute errand."

No answer.

After a few minutes of this one-way conversation, my son walked down the hall to his room, thinking of the several places he had planned to go in the car in the days to come. The next day he avoided me completely.

Two days later, the two of us found ourselves looking into an empty refrigerator. We were hungry and were the only ones home.

"Let's go out to eat," I suggested. Reluctantly, he got into my car, the thought of food overriding his lingering displeasure with me.

As we drove down the street, I handed him the car keys, saying, "Sometimes I make really dumb mistakes like I did when I took away your car keys without listening to what you were going to tell me. That wasn't fair. I wanted you to learn about responsibility—but I should have listened first. Can we erase the past couple of days and start over?"

My teenager reluctantly agreed, explaining that he had started to apologize when I interrupted him. He had stopped to help a friend and time had slipped away. He went on to say that when I interrupted him, he was about to promise to be more responsible.

I felt like a quarterback watching the films of a lost game who sees for the first time an open receiver in the end zone who could have caught a winning pass. It's always easier to know what to do when you look backward.

A Minnesota mom told me about an experience she had with one of her children—another example of speaking before listening.

"Our son brought a friend home from school on one of those days when I didn't feel like having my children around, let alone others. I embarrassed him by asking why he brought a friend home."

"He just stood there, staring off into space as I went on about what a mess the house was, that I had a headache and had a lot to do. A couple of weeks later he asked if he could miss school to go to the funeral of his friend's mother who had died of cancer."

"You can imagine how I felt when I learned it was the mother of the boy who wanted to hang out at our place—but who went home when he didn't feel welcome."

She went on to tell me how much she wished she had taken time to listen before saying anything.

LISTEN EVEN WHEN THEY CHATTER

It's not always easy to listen to children. Sometimes they go on and on, chattering about nothing.

"Yesterday, I realized my five-year-old had been talking forever, and I didn't have a clue what she had said," a mother told me.

When you're busy and a child rambles on about every detail of something, it's hard to stay tuned in. When youngsters talk, they expect us to listen. We get upset when they don't listen to us, but we often forget how important it is for *us* to listen to *them*. When we pay attention to things that don't seem very important, we'll also pick up things that are.

LISTENING OPENS THE DOOR FOR TEACHING MOMENTS

Another mom told me about her six-year-old daughter, who wanted to talk with her about a little boy who lived down the street. Being busy, it was easier to brush it off than to stop and listen.

That night when the mom was reading in bed, the six-year-old came trooping into her room and tried again. "I really need to tell you about this boy," the little girl persisted. The mother was so interested in her book that she almost sent her daughter back to bed. But the six-year-old went on to tell her mother that the little boy had wanted her to do something that wasn't right.

The little girl seemed to know that what he wanted her to do wasn't a good idea—but she had lots of questions. Since then, because of that visit, she and her mom have had many talks together about boys, girls, dating, love, and marriage.

What did the mom say to the little girl that opened the door to these future teaching moments? She just told her that anytime she wanted to talk, she would be there for her.

"HELLO, DAD, ARE YOU THERE?"

Fathers often are not very good listeners either—especially when reading the paper or watching a ball game.

When you listen to your child, be sure to do more than just pretend to listen. Have you ever had a boss who looks like he's listening—and doesn't really hear what you say? If he had really listened, he would have understood that you had a pretty good idea. And when people don't listen to us, we can't help but feel hurt. Children feel this way too.

THERE'S A TIME TO TEACH AND A TIME TO BE QUIET

We certainly need to stand up for what's right. But there are good, better, best, poor, and worse ways—and times—to teach your children right from wrong. The time to teach is when a child is ready to listen. The time to be quiet is when you know a kid's ears are turned off. But are youngsters ever *ready to listen?* Yes, they are. And it may take some patience to wait for that right time.

Suppose that your teenager is standing in the kitchen with some of her friends and, to impress them, pops off some comment with which you totally disagree. It may be about a very important value that you've been striving to teach. But in your own home—in front of her friends—out comes this provocative statement.

DON'T BE TOO QUICK WITH RIGHT ANSWERS

When a young person expresses an opinion that contradicts an important value, the natural urge is to jump in and set the youngster straight. And sometimes this is exactly what you need to do. But often there's a better way than bluntly telling a kid that she's dead wrong—especially in front of friends. It makes sense to avoid a big confrontation.

This doesn't mean that we should agree with something that's wrong. But be careful not to slam the door on communication by rushing to be right.

Especially when a teenager challenges an important value, most of us want to set things straight right then—along with the captive audience of the friends, who probably also need the wise insight we could share with them. Well, depending upon the youngster, the friends, and our relationship with both of them, we might be able to pull this off. But more often in this setting, it's better to ask if the kids would rather have root beer floats or banana splits. This is not the time to set the record straight by pointing out the foolishness of a teenager's comment. This is a time to be quiet—about that.

Correcting a teenager in front of her friends is embarrassing. And there's a good chance that well-intended words will backfire. Instead, file this topic away for future reference. This is the kind of thing to talk about in privacy. But there's more to it than talking in privacy. Talking about values that are being challenged in trial-balloon statements is something to do at just the right time. Do it when you and your teen are both calm. Do it when you can set the stage. You might want to do something fun together—go out to eat, go on a picnic, or take a hike. And before you try to slam-dunk your message about whatever value or situation needs explaining, talk about something the youngster has done that's really good. If you work hard at it, you'll usually be able to sense when a youngster will listen. Even then, don't set up a battle. Listen first, and start out by explaining that you understand where she's coming from.

Teaching values is extremely important. It takes all the skill you can muster. But don't let this frighten you off from doing it. Be yourself. Be sincere. Give your explanation as softly as you can, from the heart.

Another mistake most of us make is giving a long lecture to be sure kids get what we want them to know. But giving a long lecture is one of the worst ways to teach what's right—especially in the heat of the moment without listening. I'm an expert about giving long lectures to kids—because I've given so many of them. And I must say that few have been very effective.

If a youngster tells you that she hates school and isn't ever going back, instead of arguing, you might want to say something like, "It sounds like something terrible happened at school today."

With a nonthreatening response like this, you may get an answer like, "I didn't do anything and my teacher screamed at me."

Then you might say, "You don't think it's fair for a teacher to scream at you?"

This may open the door for a youngster to continue, "It isn't—'cause all I did was push Eric away when he grabbed me."

How to keep the info coming

We can learn far more by responding in a way that keeps a youngster talking instead of arguing. In the conflicts I've observed in family counseling, speaking before understanding is almost always part of the problem.

So listen to kids. Don't interrupt. Don't jump in too quickly with logical answers and perfect solutions. Listen. Understand. Be sincere. You don't have to agree to understand. But kids need to know you really care about them or you won't get very far.

SOME THINGS ARE NONNEGOTIABLE

We certainly don't want to leave our kids to grope in the dark about what's right or wrong. We don't want to be wishy-washy. Some things are not debatable. Some things are not negotiable. Children *will* wear a seat belt in the car. Toddlers are *not* allowed to run into a busy street. Children go to school. Drugs and drinking are *not* permitted in our home.

After asking, "What do you think about it?" listen carefully and keep the youngster talking. He or she may come up with the same conclusion you would. If this doesn't happen, you can talk about it in more detail.

SOMETIMES KIDS REALLY WANT YOU TO SAY "NO"

Young children and teenagers can't have or do everything they want whenever they feel like it. They may ask permission to do things they really don't want to do, feeling they have to ask because of what their friends may think—all the while hoping you'll rescue them by saying no.

You may want to toss the ball back in the youngster's court—along with the responsibility. "You probably have a pretty good idea of how I feel about it, but this is one of those times when you have to think about the consequences and choose for yourself."

On the other hand, sometimes we can teach, persuade, urge, and try to convince teenagers to make right choices, but if they are determined to make what we would consider a bad decision, we may not be able to do anything about it.

This is scary.

Sometimes it's better to just say, "No," which is a very good word. We shouldn't be afraid to use it, even though it will sometimes cause a conflict. It may be better to put off an answer until you can get together as parents and talk about the situation.

You won't ever stop worrying about the serious consequences of the decisions your children might make. A very real concern is that if we give our children permission to make a decision, it will seem like we have given permission to do something that is contrary to our values.

It isn't easy to teach responsibility without practice. And even if we don't openly give this responsibility, older children and teenagers often take it anyway. So there's a fine balance.

A young person's career interests may be quite different than what parents may have in mind. And as much as we may want a child to go into computer programming, medicine, accounting, or law, if he or she wants to do something else, that's what counts. It's the youngster's life. Of course we would hope a career choice is honorable and honest. Sure, there are lots of things to consider—including income and security. It's appropriate to ask questions and to stimulate thought and discussion—without pushing a son or daughter to choose a job path that he or she wouldn't like.

Don't give kids permission to do self-destructive things

But what about influencing children and teenagers on matters of principle? We should never give children permission to do things that will hurt them—like smoking, drinking, drugs, pornography, or sex. But even when parents teach children what's right, some of them will still make big mistakes. At least we shouldn't make it easier for them to make the mistakes.

Imagine a mother telling her fifteen-year-old daughter to clean her room or the daughter could forget about having her boyfriend spend the night. A prominent writer tells this story about herself in a book about teen behavior and coming of age.[7]

Get the picture? This teenager was too immature to clean her room without being hounded. But swallowing the illogical standards of the day, her mother was more concerned about her daughter's boyfriend's seeing her messy room than she was about his sleeping over.

OUR LISTENING HELPS THEIR THINKING

When we listen to understand, it's surprising how often children and teens figure out good answers. When we listen, frustrations tumble out. Without being scolded or put down, a child may conclude that school isn't so bad after all. A great teacher and friend, George Durrant, who knows something about kids from raising eight children and working with countless thousands of others, explained it this way: "I have gradually learned that my children do not want my ready-made, time-proven, and wise answers. At least they do not want such answers immediately. To them, being able to ask their questions and talk about their problems is more important than receiving my answers. Usually when they get through talking, if I have listened long and well enough, they really don't need my answer. They have already found their answer."

By the way, even though these parenting skills work, don't expect them to be a part of your life by ten o'clock tonight. It's like learning to drive a car, fly a plane, or work a computer. They sound easy, but doing them right is another matter.

At first, trying to drive a car is a little rough. But once the skills are repeated over and over, you don't have to think about them. They just happen. And to some degree, the same is true about raising children.

---

[7] Naomi Wolff, *Promiscuities: The Secret Struggle for Womanhood* (New York: Fawcett Books, August 1998).

It won't be easy—but you are going to be an even more effective parent than you already are.

You may remember the age-old poem about the wise old owl:

> *A wise old owl sat on an oak.*
> *The more he saw, the less he spoke.*
> *The less he spoke, the more he heard.*
> *Why can't we be like that wise old bird?*[8]

So why can't we be like that wise old bird? I don't know. But I wish I had been. Blurting out frustrations, punishments, right answers, and perfect solutions was one of my worst failings as a parent. Maybe if I write "Don't say much until you listen" a bunch of times, it will sink in so I won't make this mistake again—or at least as often.

> *Don't say much until you listen!*
> *Don't say much until you listen!*
> *Don't say much until you listen!*
> *Don't say much until you listen!*
> *Don't say much until you listen!*
> *Don't say much until you listen!*
> *Don't say much until you listen!*
> *Don't say much until you listen!*
> *Don't say much until you listen!*

KEYS TO RAISING CHILDREN
1. **Take charge as a friend—not the enemy.**
2. **Make home a happy place to be.**
3. **Give your children something priceless— your time.**
4. **Don't say much until you listen.**

[8] Anonymous

5

Teach Them the "Rules of Life"

Ve often think that our job as parents is to *tell* kids things, and most of us do lots of *telling*. But this isn't our job. The plain fact is that *telling isn't teaching*, and our job is to *teach*—not *tell*. Good car salesmen, teachers, and parents do more than *tell* facts.

Think about it. If a car salesman is really good, is it because he *tells* people more facts than someone else? Probably not. The best salespeople are those who are effective teachers. You can *tell* people lots of facts without doing any teaching, and there's a big difference.

HOW TO TEACH VALUES

Teaching goes beyond giving facts. Teaching includes whatever it takes to get someone to soak in and accept what you've explained. Thus, an effective teacher is an effective opinion leader. A person who teaches communicates information in a way that convinces someone to do something, to change direction, or to strengthen or weaken a particular belief. But this can't be done simply by giving out facts. Not understanding this is a big mistake most parents, teachers, managers, communicators, and other professionals make all the time. So how do you go about selling a car to a customer, ideas to the public, or values to a youngster?

FIRST, BE A FRIEND

Suppose you wanted to buy a car, and the salesman sat you down and, without much feeling, gave you a lecture about the car he thought you should have. This would probably turn you off so that you wouldn't even hear what he was trying to tell you—even if what he was saying was right. That's why good salespeople don't do this. The first thing they do is inspire trust by becoming a friend. People are much more likely to buy something from someone they like than from someone they don't like.

Some salespeople are very good at inspiring trust and confidence. Others are not. Some try, but their attempt to be friendly comes through as syrupy and artificial. This doesn't work either. On the other hand, a really good salesperson cares about his customer and comes across as a friend.

SECOND, FIGURE OUT NEEDS

Part of establishing confidence in a customer is showing enough interest to help the person figure out what he or she needs. But people often don't know what they need and sometimes don't even know what they think they want. This is what makes marketing, managing, leading, and parenting so challenging. Becoming a friend and helping children to figure out their needs are the first two steps in teaching values.

But helping youngsters figure out their needs doesn't mean sitting back while they figure out life for themselves. Life is too important and too complicated to push a youngster out into the world with the charge to "figure it out." Our job is to teach kids what's right and wrong. And in spite of what some may say, some things are right and some things are wrong.

THIRD, HELP SOLVE PROBLEMS

Once a friendly salesperson has established a relationship of confidence and has a pretty good idea about needs, he's in a good position to help solve your problems. He knows something about you. He understands your needs. And he's ready to help you solve your problem. That's what selling, managing, and parenting is all about.

THE "RULES OF LIFE"

Parents want their children to grow up to be happy and successful. They want to help their kids learn what it takes to accomplish something good in life. Parents also want to help their youngsters avoid the mistakes they made while growing up and others they now know would be risky or hazardous. Parents basically want to teach their kids how to play life's game—in other words, to teach them the "rules of life."

TIME-TESTED PRINCIPLES

There are some basic principles, or laws, about life and the world around us. These time-tested principles are the "rules of life." The principles are basic truths. It doesn't matter what you or I happen to think about them. They don't need to be voted on, because truth is truth. These basic principles have been around for centuries and are time-tested laws.

Every person is free to choose whether to follow them or not. Of course, whether or not we follow them will always result in consequences. Some of these consequences will be immediate and some may not be. Some of the consequences are good and some are bad.

Well, if life's that simple, what are these all-important principles? What are these "rules of life?" And why doesn't everyone know them so that everyone is happy and successful?

Good questions.

LOTS OF MISINFORMATION OUT THERE

The problem is that along with these time-tested principles, there are lots of fuzzy theories and flagrant untruths that get in the way. All of this misinformation makes life interesting, challenging, and difficult for everyone—even for those who are wise and have had plenty of experience with the ups and downs of life.

If it's difficult for people with knowledge and experience to know the facts, think of how difficult it is for a youngster to sort out correct principles from all the misinformation that's around. Children need parents to help them sort things out. And helping them do this is one of our biggest responsibilities.

SOME "RULES OF LIFE" ARE OBVIOUS TO EVERYONE

Some "rules of life" are obvious. We need oxygen to live. We also need water and food. These are clear and basic facts. With these basics, in the right amounts, we live. Without them, we die.

Other basic principles include warnings about certain dangers. Fingers on very hot metal will get burned. Someone in the middle of the ocean without a lifeboat or a quick rescue is not going to live very long. Likewise, being dropped off a cliff at a significant altitude is not compatible with long life. You can think of dozens of other examples of things that have obviously dire or deadly consequences—some immediate and some gradual.

Children learn and discover some "rules of life" quite readily while others are more difficult to recognize and discern. The consequence of choosing to work may result in earning enough to eat while choosing not to work may leave you hungry. One of the consequences of stealing may be spending time in jail. The consequence of driving a car at a high speed on a city street may be getting a ticket and a fine—or worse.

But the consequences of not following other "rules of life" may not be so obvious. Not teaching a child the basic "rules of life" is like expecting a youngster to play a violin with no instruction. Kids need and deserve instructions, maps, and compasses.

WHAT PRINCIPLES ARE IMPORTANT
FOR YOUR FAMILY?

The question is, which instructions, maps, and compasses are your kids going to receive? And where are they going to get them? They can get information from lots of places—the kid down the street, what they see on television, things they find on the Internet, school, and you. Obviously some of the information kids pick up from these sources is excellent. Some isn't. That's why your children have you.

You may want to get your family together to discuss what your family is all about. You can define its purpose just like a company does in a mission statement.[9] After you've received everyone's input and thought about it for a while, it might look something like this:

> *Our family is a special group of people who love each other, help each other learn the "rules of life," have fun, work together to provide income and other needs, solve problems, pray together, and help others.*

Although you may wonder how to get your family to brainstorm about its purpose, once you do you'll be surprised at the good results. And as you talk about the purpose of your family, the opportunity will open up to talk about faith, the purpose of life, and the "rules of life" as you see them.

HOW IMPORTANT IS RELIGION?

Having a spiritual life is very important to my family. We pray together every day. We give thanks, pray about our problems,

---

[9] The concept of the family mission statement is explained in detail by Stephen R. Covey in *The 7 Habits of Highly Successful Families* (New York: Golden Books, 1998).

and pray for our children. We read from the scriptures together. Several of our children do this better with their children than we did. Even the little ones who can't read take a turn, repeating a few words their parents read for them.

I hope you take your children with you to worship services and other religious activities. This will supplement your teachings about the differences between right and wrong and increase the likelihood that your children will make friends with others who have strong values. If a child learns that he or she is a child of God, with high expectations, he or she has a basic reason not to follow the crowd.

A mother called in to Dr. Laura Schlessinger's radio program, thinking she could teach her child to be honest and good without religion. Dr. Laura asked what she would do when her youngster got older and challenged her authority. When the mother didn't have an answer, Dr. Laura explained that without religion, children don't know there's a *higher authority,* and without recognizing a *higher authority* they are likely to rationalize almost any kind of behavior.

One of the big problems in the world today is that people make up their own rules—rules of convenience and comfort that deny any higher authority. But there is a higher authority. And there are ten "rules of life" that have been taught in one form or another in every successful culture throughout history. These rules are not recorded as suggestions, and no society I know of has ever survived without them.

MURDER, RAPE, AND ASSAULT ARE NOT RIGHT AND HAVE DIRE CONSEQUENCES

Certainly this basic "rule of life" should be taught to children in every family. But don't they just know this? They should, from the thing we call conscience. But think about the thousands of violent events most kids see on the screen during their growing-up years. Few would doubt that seeing so much violence is partially responsible for many of these terrible crimes; it is so desensitizing that even good kids are more likely to fight and quarrel. So, besides cutting down on the violence kids see on television and videos, they need to be taught specifically that violent behavior is not acceptable. Likewise, children need to be taught the sanctity of life and a revulsion for killing the unborn. Abortion is a terrible way to deal with inconvenient or unwanted pregnancies.

DISOBEYING LAWS RESULTS IN CONSEQUENCES THAT LIMIT FREEDOM

Kids need to know it's unacceptable to shoplift, break speed limits, drive recklessly, or violate the law in any way. There's more to this than simply teaching children about the laws of their community and country. There's even more to it than teaching that violations of law may result in fines, losing driving privileges, or spending time in jail. Children need to be taught principles of right and wrong—and how to listen to their conscience.

USING ALCOHOL, DRUGS, AND TOBACCO IS SELF-DESTRUCTIVE

Almost everyone agrees that substance abuse is a problem, but some people think that kids learn enough about these prohibitions in school. Well, if they did, we wouldn't have such problems with them. The answer is clear. We need to do a better job of teaching kids not to use harmful substances. And this needs to start at home—through example as well as through good learning experiences shared in a family.

Unfortunately, teaching the consequences of using these substances is not enough. Every school kid knows that smoking will eventually cause lung cancer, heart disease, and/or emphysema. Yet countless kids start smoking every week because they want to be *in* with friends who use this stuff, telling themselves "it won't happen to me."

Many kids get hooked on these substances simply because if they don't join their friends, they will be called "chicken." One way to help kids learn how to respond to such pressure is in a roll-play activity where one youngster practices saying no to an invitation to smoke (or drink or use drugs) while others taunt him for being "chicken." As you get kids to figure out that the person who says no is the smart one, it helps them see how foolish it is to go along with the crowd. And it will also teach them how to respond when they are put in these situations.

HONEST WORK CAN PROVIDE SECURITY AND FULFILL NEEDS

Unfortunately, many kids don't know how to work these days. They don't need to work because their parents hand them big allowances, toys, bikes, cars, and the gas to run them without expecting much, if any, effort in return. This isn't wise. Kids need to learn to work. They also need to learn that the right kind of work is a joy, and that by studying, preparing, and working they can have the things they need in life.

TREATING OTHERS WITH RESPECT IS A PREREQUISITE TO BEING TREATED WELL

Throughout history, when people respect themselves, one another, and one another's belongings, there is generally contentment. When people don't respect themselves, one another, or another's property, there is discontent, disagreements, fighting, and sometimes even war.

Kids learn best from copying the behavior of those around them. Whom do your children look up to? Who are their heroes and heroines? Hopefully, in addition to you, their grandparents, and other good role models in your family, you can help your children find great heroes and heroines in books.

But as kids copy the disrespect they see carried out by peers at school and in dysfunctional families in sitcoms and on videos, it's no surprise that many treat one another, parents, and teachers with disrespect. It's not easy to override all this negative behavior, but it's important to try. Zero tolerance for parental disrespect is a beginning. But this also means that we need to respect our kids, which isn't always easy—especially when they've been obnoxious to us. Respect should be a frequent topic for family discussion.

HONESTY RESULTS IN TRUST, AND DISHONESTY IN CONSEQUENCES

Teaching honesty starts with being honest. Example. Example. Example. You can also teach honesty through stories and books that build character.

But how can you find these stories? "A simple rule of thumb is to look for books in which the main character grows. As your child becomes involved with the protagonist, he vicariously shares in that character's development. Just as a child learns from real experiences, he can also learn from vicarious ones—and far more safely. Do we want our children to know what honesty means? Then we might teach them about Abe Lincoln walking three miles to return six cents, and conversely about Aesop's shepherd boy who cried wolf."[10] This profound advice comes from an excellent resource for finding value-filled fiction and biographies of great people that can add to a child's experience about character.

What if you picked a "character of the week" to talk about at mealtimes? Some families help their children develop character by telling stories and talking about a "character of the week"

[10] William Kilpatrick, Gregory and Suzanne M. Wolfe, *Books That Build Character* (New York: Touchstone Books, 1994).

such as cheerfulness, happiness, prudence, self-control, and chastity.[11]

SAVE SEX FOR MARRIAGE

Is it even realistic to think kids may wait until they are married to have sex? Yes, it is. There's a much better chance that they will wait if we have high expectations. But if we have low expectations, they will probably meet them.

If you think that sex should be saved for marriage, as I firmly do, you can do three things to decrease the likelihood of your kids getting prematurely involved in sexual activity:[12]

1. Let your kids know that sex is only for marriage.
2. Discourage steady dating.
3. Provide parental monitoring.

When a child of any age asks questions about sex, stop what you're doing and clearly answer the question. Use teaching moments like this to explain that sex is reserved only for people married to each other.

At the appropriate time and place, explain exactly what you expect—no sexual intercourse until marriage. Also explain that controlling sexual urges means avoiding situations where it's easy to lose control. This means being in safe places instead of unsafe places. It also means not touching one another's private body parts, or engaging in other activities that can lead to intercourse.

Although it's not always possible to know where kids go and who they are with, it helps to set family rules about dating. Optimally, it's best to put off dating until age sixteen. Waiting to date

[11] Thomas Lickona, Ph.D., *Educating for Character* (New York: Bantam Books, 1992).
[12] Sexual Health Today, a slide program and lecture notes created by the Medical Institute for Sexual Health, Austin, Texas.

until the later teen years and avoiding steady dating reduces the risk of early sexual involvement. But how do you get your kids to buy into family rules like this when their friends don't have such limits? Agree that your family is different and help them learn to feel that being distinctive is honorable. This isn't easy, but it gives young people an identity—a sense of belonging. When family ties are strong, children are less likely to look for identity with a gang or with friends who get into trouble.

Parents should also know where kids are and be around when they are around. Parental monitoring helps, because kids who hang out together too much can get into trouble even at home in the middle of the afternoon. A good family rule is that a parent needs to be at home whenever kids get together.

FOUR MAIN MESSAGES TO TEACH KIDS ABOUT SEX

Most of us are reluctant to say very much to our children about sex. It's something that seems too private to talk about. What would we say? And surely they've been taught about these things in school. Well, you're right that sex has been talked about in school. Actually, more has probably been said than you would like. The trouble is that unless you are very fortunate about what is taught in your schools regarding sex, it's taught without values. Without values? That's right. Sadly, kids are taught about the mechanics—along with ways some think sex can be made safe. The truth is that nonmarried sex isn't safe for kids—or for anyone. And unfortunately, with all the talk and sex education classes, teen pregnancies and sexually transmitted disease rates have increased. If you don't teach your kids these very important points, no one will. So what are these important points?

1. Save sex for marriage.
2. In married sex you can give and receive pleasure, trust, and love.

3. Condoms and pills don't protect from many risks of unmarried sex.
4. Say no to requests for nonmarried sex.

It really isn't all that difficult to explain these things to kids. When my kids were growing up, we explained how things worked pretty well and we talked about saving sex for marriage—but I didn't say much about the other three points. I think I covered them in roundabout ways—but I certainly didn't say, "Okay, there are four things I want you to know about sex—and here they are, one, two, three, and four." And this is exactly what I'd suggest that you do.

1. SAVE SEX FOR MARRIAGE

Why? Personal values. Family values. Religious values. It's the right thing to do. It's a "rule of life."

This is so important that I hope you will encourage your kids to make a written commitment to wait until marriage to have sex. Hundreds of thousands of young folks have made such commitments, verbally and in writing, in True Love Waits and other excellent youth programs.

Teenagers who make such a commitment are much more likely to remain abstinent than their peers during these vulnerable years. There's no question that having friends with similar values and being involved in youth groups that promote high standards of character and chastity are very helpful. Do everything you can to get your kids to make such a promise to themselves, to you, and to their future marriage partner.

Teaching kids about character and waiting works

Teaching young people about character and waiting for marriage works. Among girls who belong to a Best Friends group in Washington, D.C., only 10.2 percent failed to keep their commitment to wait for sex. Compare this to 81.4 percent of their

---

peers who had experienced sex by the end of the twelfth grade.[13] "There was a lot of pressure on me to have sex," a cute African-American girl told us. She said that everyone around her was "doing it—but I'm not," she proudly added.

It's largely up to you to counter the dangerous message kids are getting that it's all right to play around with sex—as long as no one gets pregnant. The only safe sex is in a faithful marriage. This is what we should be teaching our children.

2. IN MARRIED SEX YOU CAN GIVE AND RECEIVE PLEASURE, TRUST, AND LOVE

Sex itself is not bad. In fact, at the right time and circumstance, sex is not only good, but very good. Young people need to know this. They also need to know that sex is pleasurable and, with consideration in marriage, very appropriate. From watching movies and television, kids get the idea that sex is alluring, breathtaking, and terrific. In many respects they get a distorted idea about what to expect. And unfortunately most kids today don't get a very good idea of the wholesome bond that sex can be in a marriage where there is trust and true love. Explain this to your kids in the right way, at the right times, and in the right doses. As you talk, here are some points you will probably want to include:

- Saving sex for marriage builds trust.
- Your own partner is worth waiting for.
- Waiting till you're married makes sex even more special.
- The right thing to do is to wait for sex until marriage.

[13] Rowberry, David R., An Evaluation of the Washington, D.C. Best Friends Program, a thesis submitted to the Faculty of the Graduate School at the University of California in fulfillment of requirements for the degree of Doctor of Philosophy, Department of Education, 1995.

3. CONDOMS AND PILLS DON'T PROTECT FROM MANY RISKS OF UNMARRIED SEX

Condoms don't provide the *safe sex* that's been promised. Did you know that they provide almost no protection against some types of sexually transmitted diseases and poor protection from others? Dr. Tom Fitch, an expert about this problem, puts it this way: "There is no responsible sex for unmarried adolescents."

Flawed message

Unfortunately, kids are getting the message that they can have sex if it's "responsible"—meaning if they remember to use a condom. But since sex with condoms isn't really safe, is this the best thing we can teach kids? I don't think so. Here are some facts you can use to correct the flawed message that is being sold to the public—and your kids:

• Birth control pills give no protection from STDs

Another flawed idea is to give girls birth control pills, shots, or implants. Birth control doesn't provide any protection at all from sexually transmitted diseases—none, zero. Think about it. Teenagers on the pill are 100 percent vulnerable to AIDS and every other sexually transmitted disease. So they are told to use condoms, too. But 95 percent of the girls on birth control pills don't use condoms. This means only 5 percent do! Five percent! What kind of public health program is that?

• Condoms don't protect against chlamydia

Condoms don't do a good job of protecting against chlamydia, which causes pelvic inflammatory disease, abdominal pain, and sterility. To make it worse, chlamydia has become more and more difficult to treat.

- **Genital herpes and venereal wart viruses get around condoms**

Condoms give poor protection from genital herpes and venereal warts. This is frightening because venereal warts are the cause of almost all cervical cancer, and although medications can help control genital herpes, no medicine can cure it or venereal warts. These infections last a lifetime.

What does poor protection against pregnancy tell us about STDs?

About 16 percent of teenage girls relying on condoms will be pregnant in a year. Girls can get pregnant only a few days a month—but they are a target for AIDS, genital herpes, and chlamydia every day, every month.

Even so, kids are being told that *if they can't wait,* to use a condom. This is like telling kids never to steal a car, but if they do to wear a seat belt! Here we are with an explosive epidemic of sexually transmitted diseases and instead of teaching kids about values, character, and waiting till marriage, a flawed condom program encourages and enables kids to continue this self-defeating behavior.

4. Say no to requests for nonmarried sex

Instead of teaching kids to take along a condom, "just in case," coach them how to say *no,* and mean it. Teach them to not let it happen. A good family activity is to get kids to figure out creative ways to confidently and firmly say no so they'll have a good answer when someone suggests they have sex:

- What part of "no" don't you understand?
- Not now. Not in a little while. Not tomorrow. Not next week. Not until I'm with the person I'm married to.
- I said no and I mean it.

- No marriage, no sex.
- *Nyet* is "no" in Russian. Do you need it translated?
- I made a promise to wait till I'm married.
- I'm out of here.

Confident kids can say such things. It takes courage—but this is what character is all about. Help kids to know that when a date, or friend, or anyone asks for sex, it's time to go. This is not something to stick around to discuss. It's nonnegotiable. Help kids to know that they don't owe a date anything—certainly not sex, or even an apology for saying *no*. Kristine Napier, a wise health educator and writer, tells kids: "Don't apologize or think you're wimpy for walking away from a steamy situation. Walking away actually requires an incredible amount of strength. Sometimes removing yourself from the situation may be the only way to make your date understand. It will also help your date realize you're not kidding."[14]

Practicing refusal skills can be a very worthwhile activity. There's no question that peer pressure is tough. But thinking ahead about how to respond can really help a teen or preteen who may be pressured to be touched, undressed, or involved in other sexual situations.

Teaching children these things reminds me of an interesting New York City traffic sign that says:

NO PARKING
Not for 10 minutes
Not for 10 seconds
Not at all!

[14] Kristine Napier, *The Power of Abstinence* (New York: Avon Books, 1996).

Now is the time to teach children absolutes. Some things are just plain no. Not for ten minutes. Not for ten seconds. Not at all!

Warn kids about sexual abuse

Although this may not be likely in your family, the tragic reality is that far too many young people are sexually abused. Carefully, without causing unneeded mistrust or alarm, caution children not to allow anyone, male or female, friend, relative, or stranger, to touch any of their private body parts. Let them know this is unacceptable—and that you want to know should anyone ever try to bother them in any way.

GETTING TOGETHER
WITH YOUR FAMILY

You can share some of these things with a youngster when you're on an activity together, some in little snippets of time when teaching moments come up, and others when your family is all together. Just do it.

Many families have a little devotional at supper time. Others have a family night once a week when they get together, have a brief spiritual or motivational thought, time to talk, sometimes a game, and a special treat.

With or without anything very structured, you can do some very effective teaching when you get your family together long enough to sit down for a meal. It takes even more effort to generate meaningful mealtime conversations, but it's worth it. Think of the benefits of talking together about what's happening at school, at work, and in the world. Ask each member of the family to tell you about their day. Ask each child to teach you something he or she learned in school that day. You'll be surprised at some of the interesting things you'll learn. Other times you'll discover things in these debriefings that a youngster has picked up at school or elsewhere that you'll want to correct. Even though traditional family mealtimes are less frequent now, I think you'll find them a big help.

LIFE DOESN'T COME WITH GUARANTEES
But what if, after all you do, a youngster doesn't accept what you try to teach? Sadly, this happens sometimes. Some kids will break our rules. Some kids will break our hearts. But many will listen and appreciate what you are trying to do. In fact, most children prefer a happy, structured home with rules to one that's unstructured and permissive.

It comes back to being a friend. If children think you are a friend who really cares, chances are they will be receptive to most of the insights about life you share with them.

But to get close to our kids, we need to spend time with them. I can't promise that if you invest a certain amount of time with a youngster, everything will turn out perfectly. Life doesn't come with this kind of guarantee. Sometimes even when you do everything right, sad things may happen. But spending time with kids is a solid investment. In other words, sometimes the market goes down—and sometimes kids disappoint us.

A strong friendship with a child may or may not continue over the years. But when difficult times come, it helps to have some reserves, built with deposits of love over the years.

Keep in mind, no matter how hard you try or what you do, you'll have your share of problems. But *being a friend* and teaching your children the "rules of life" will help you be a more effective parent.

KEYS TO RAISING CHILDREN

1. Take charge as a friend—not the enemy.
2. Make home a happy place to be.
3. Give children something priceless—your time.
4. Don't say much until you listen.
5. Teach them the "rules of life."

6

Get Help from Your Spouse or a Friend

If you were running a school, would you try to do it alone? If you were the president of a large corporation, would you make all of the decisions yourself? Or if you were a high-school coach, would you try to solve all of the problems without any help? Some may try to do any one of these alone—but I doubt that many who try are very successful. And no one solos in a 747.

The same idea applies to running a family and raising children. Even with lots of training and experience with young children and teenagers, I couldn't do it alone. There are too many tough decisions and too many variables. Anyway, I believe the old saying that two heads are better than one.

SOLVING PROBLEMS TOGETHER

Parenting is tough, really tough, even when there are two parents under the same roof who work well together. And two people seldom start out with all the same ideas about how to raise children. Quite often one parent is more firm and rigid while the other is soft and understanding. Although these differences are sometimes annoying, when parents can work together these different points of view can keep a family from getting too far off-balance.

SET SOLID GROUND RULES FOR YOUR FAMILY

You can set standards and basic ground rules for your family in your own little management meetings. This is your family. It's your home. Being in charge, you can set the tone for your home.

Obviously there are effective and ineffective ways to do this. But it's really up to you to decide what your home will be like. As the two of you decide the ground rules, you will be a strong influence in the lives of your children. Decide the principles between the two of you—and then involve the children in making rules for the family.

For example, as discussed earlier, a common problem when children are young is how to get them to bed at night and then how to get them to stay there. When parents think a youngster is settled in bed with the door closed, a child may show up asking for a drink, another story, or to get in bed with them.

When this happens one parent may think it's necessary to give an extra hug or another drink—or to let the child get in bed with them. The other may think that once a kid is in bed, that's it.

A mom and dad meeting is a great place to coordinate the strategy for handling this problem. Having a game plan in place with both parents in on the play makes success and family harmony much more likely.

Meetings to run a company or a family

If managers, board of directors, military staff, and coaches need to have meetings to solve problems, it makes sense for parents to do the same thing to solve problems in a family.

BUT WHAT ABOUT SINGLE PARENTS?

Single parents can use the same strategy to fit their needs—getting together regularly with a friend or another single parent to help solve problems that come up with their children. Frequently, as they review current problems, they figure out

---

strategies to prevent future problems. Many single parents have told me about teaming up with someone with similar values to discuss problems calmly and objectively.

A mother who lost her husband to an early heart attack explained that because of the good years they had working together, she can often sense what her husband would have suggested if he could be there. Even with this help, she soon learned it was difficult to be an effective parent all by herself. So she found a friend that she could talk with about her children, which she did every week or so—and more often when problems arose.

Parenting is such a big job that even when a single parent has lots of experience, it helps to talk with someone regularly about decisions in dealing with the everyday problems.

You never get it all figured out. Each child is different.

So is each parent.

THREE-STEP PROBLEM-SOLVING

When a television talk show host asked me what parents could do to be more effective with their children, I answered, "three-step problem-solving." This concept is so incredibly simple and amazingly helpful that every parent can, and should, do it. In fact, you probably already do it most of the time. I'm just suggesting that you do it more regularly to solve and prevent problems in your home.

So, what are the three steps of *three-step problem-solving?*

- Get together privately.
- Think together.
- Make the best decision you can.

STEP 1: GET TOGETHER PRIVATELY

Most fathers, and many mothers, can remember at least one experience of coming home after a terrible day at work to find things at home were also completely out of control. I can certainly remember such a day. Before I even opened the door I could hear someone crying. When I came in it didn't take long to realize that my tough day at work was nothing compared to what had been going on at home. The place was a mess. Kids were fighting. My wife was trying to fix dinner. One of the girls wanted to go to a sleepover. The toilet had overflowed.

Things kept getting worse. While I was pushing a plunger in the toilet, my wife told me that the washer had quit working. In the midst of this confusion we tried to talk about the sleepover. And during all the commotion, the daughter who wanted to go to the sleepover was pushier than a professional lobbyist.

Trying to make good decisions about something like a sleepover when the household is in a state of crisis usually doesn't work. We shouldn't have even considered the sleepover question right then. We made the mistake of trying to talk about it at the wrong time, in the wrong place, and with too many listening ears. It's much better to consider a decision like this privately—without children butting in with their opinions.

Where can parents talk about things like this in private?

It doesn't matter where you go to escape the chaos—as long as you do. You could go for a walk together. Or maybe you would rather go for a ride. Other times you may want to go out to eat so that you can talk. You may want to sit in the park and discuss a current crisis. Or you may not need to go somewhere else. You can get together at home—behind closed doors. No lobbyists. Just the two of you.

How often?

When we first realized the value of having little family management meetings, once a week worked out just about right. Sometimes we did this on Sunday afternoons or on Friday evenings when we tried to get out of the house to spend some time alone together. But sometimes a problem was too urgent to wait until the weekend. As the children started growing, this happened more often and there were more problems to talk about. Soon we were getting together for a few minutes almost every day to think through problems and decisions. And later, during times of real crisis, we sometimes found ourselves getting together two or three times a day.

Like a business

Managing a family like good managers run their businesses is just plain smart. Of course this means regular planning meetings, phone calls, frequent quick exchanges, and lots of lunch or dinner meetings.

If it makes sense for businesspeople to solve problems over lunch or dinner—especially when a big decision needs to be made—it makes sense for parents to *think together* about family problems at a getaway lunch or dinner.

One mom and dad relied on these little meetings when one of their kids was getting beaten up by a bully on the way home from school. They decided to talk with their son about ways to avoid the bully. Besides not walking alone, the father coached him to stand and walk with confidence instead of looking scared, explaining that bullies usually—not always, but often—single out little guys who look timid and frightened. They talked about when and how to walk away from bullies, even when they tease and insult you.

The boy's parents also asked their son if he would like to take karate. He did. Questions were asked and answered about choosing a good karate program where children are taught obedience, using their skills defensively, so as not to become bullies themselves.

Once you start visiting together regularly, when a youngster comes up with a tough request that needs more thought you can explain that you'll come up with an answer after you've had a chance to talk with his other parent in your mom and dad meeting. He may not like being put off, especially at first, but letting a youngster know that this is important enough for you to talk about in your parent meeting shows him that his request will be seriously considered.

If a youngster wants an answer to something immediately, let him talk about it. If you're a good listener and are lucky, he might talk himself out of it.

STEP 2: THINK TOGETHER
Raising children is so tough that parents need a plan to help solve the problems that come up every day. Otherwise they'll be frustrated all the time.

A parent can make much better decisions by *thinking together* with someone. In our family, it became obvious that we absolutely had to spend some time *thinking together* about family problems on a regular basis.

Talk about what's going on. Consider the options. Sometimes *the right thing to do* will be very clear. Sometimes it won't. Listen carefully to each other.

But what if you have different opinions? Listen more carefully to what the other has to say. Of course these discussions can turn into arguments if you let them. So don't let them. Remember, you're on the same side.

One of the early differences we had in our family was whether children should wear shoes when they went out to play. When my wife was growing up, she and her brothers and sisters went barefoot much of the time. Shoes were for going someplace special. So when our first child started playing outside, it seemed natural to my wife for our daughter to go barefoot.

I thought she should wear shoes. When I was growing up, we wore shoes all the time, unless we were swimming, taking a bath, or in bed. Listening to each other helped us understand where the other one was coming from. She explained her family's tradition to go barefoot—and I explained my family's expectation about wearing shoes. So what did we come up with? A pretty good solution. She convinced me that it was okay not to wear shoes in the house and I persuaded her that it was a good idea for kids to wear shoes outside so they wouldn't get slivers in their feet.

Thinking together can result in better answers than any one person can discover alone. That's why regular management meetings between two parents, or a parent and a friend, make so much sense.

STEP 3: MAKE THE BEST DECISION YOU CAN

This sounds easier than it often is. At some point you just have to decide to decide—and then make the best choice you can. Sometimes it comes down to making the *least worst* decision. But more often you can make a decision that you both feel good about. It also helps to pray together about important decisions regarding your children.

Some decisions are really difficult—such as the request to go to a slumber party. When a slumber party question came up, we wanted to know all about what was planned. Of course, if it had been one of those co-ed sleepovers, the answer would have been a definite no, right on the spot.

I can't imagine parents allowing boy and girl sleepovers. We don't even like single-gender sleepovers. Too many things can happen at slumber parties, even with careful monitoring and supervision.

A teenager named Jamie wanted to have a co-ed sleepover. She told her mom that no one planned to go to bed, they were just going to watch movies and play games—and if they fell asleep it would be in their clothes! Wisely, her parents said no. They decided the risks were too great. I agree. Boys and girls in pajamas, or whatever they wear at night, belong in their own homes, in their own beds. Single-gender sleepovers are a big enough worry.

So what about all-girl sleepover parties? Some of the potential problems are obvious. Others are not. Under the best circumstances, you can assume there won't be much sleep. Supervision is essential. The host parents must not only be home—but in and out of the sleeping area during the night to be sure everything is under control. On the rare times we said yes to these activities, other than in our home, we spent plenty of time talking with the other parents—and were given assurances that movies and television would meet our standards. This is not easy to do. We always preferred that if these all-night events were to happen that they be in our home. But being the host parents of a teen slumber party is a big responsibility and commitment. And it's wise to take plenty of time to talk about all the factors involved in a parent management meeting.

When there isn't a good answer
Sometimes there isn't a good answer. No matter how close parents are to each other, two people are not always going to see things the same way. The more you work at it, the more you will think alike on important matters—and when you don't, you'll be a good balance for each other.

When a decision turns out to have been a mistake, try to forget who was right or wrong and learn from the mistake without blaming each other. It's hard not to, especially if you were right and your spouse was wrong, but if you stick together and support each other, it's less likely that you'll be divided and conquered.

* * *

Three-step problem-solving really works. Use it in your family. Obviously parenting is a big, big job. It's more important than being the president of a large corporation, a high-school coach, or the principal of a school. One of the basic management tools people use to run these groups is to meet and think together. You can do this in your family. With three-step problem-solving, problems will not disappear, but they will be much easier to manage—together.

- Get together privately.
- Think together.
- Make the best decision you can.

You can't start using this helpful tool too soon.

Go for a walk or a ride—or just go into another room and close the door. Remember, no lobbyists. Just two of you—you and a spouse or a friend. And how often? At least every week—maybe every day if things are a little unsettled right now.

And in case you don't have plenty to talk about already, you'll find a few things below to help get you get started.

Happy parenting. You're on the way.

PARENTS CAN SOLVE PROBLEMS LIKE THESE ON WALKS, ON RIDES, AT LUNCH ESCAPES, ON DATES, ON LITTLE TRIPS, OR AT HOME

Bedtime problems
A youngster who thinks no one likes him
Bizarre clothing fads
A child's request to take drum lessons
Money problems
A teenager who wants to go away for spring break
A daughter's request to go to a concert
A son who says he's going to drop math
A kid who wants to go to a slumber (less) party
An *F* and two *D's*
Renting inappropriate movies

A child who has stolen money from a sibling or parent
Teaching kids to work instead of expecting handouts
A school teacher who constantly yells
This year's vacation budget
A new job opportunity—and the possibility of moving
A thirteen-year-old who wants to date
Establishing responsibility in the home
A request to get a pet skunk
Our family's purpose and goals
How to teach kids about sex and morality
The use of the family car and driving privileges
Inspirational thoughts we can share at dinner

KEYS TO RAISING CHILDREN

1. **Take charge as a friend—not the enemy.**
2. **Make home a happy place to be.**
3. **Give children something priceless—your time.**
4. **Don't say much until you listen.**
5. **Teach them the "rules of life."**
6. **Get help from your spouse or a friend.**

7

Take Time to Regroup— away from the Kids

Since you're on duty 8,760 hours a year, an important secret to living with children without losing your mind is taking time to regroup—away from the kids. Parenting is a twenty-four-hour-a-day job for seven days a week. This totals 168 hours a week, during which there isn't a minute when parents are not responsible for their children.

PARENTS NEED TIME OUT OF THE GAME
Even when children are unusually well-behaved, parents need a break. Parents need to get out, away, gone for a little while every week. You don't see many basketball players on the court every minute of a game. Even the best players can't stay in the heat of the game without some rest. And this applies to parents too.

But I think this means more than just time off the court. When a basketball player gets tired, a sub replaces the exhausted player while he rests for a few minutes on the bench. Then, after catching his breath, he's back in the game, refreshed and ready to play. Many parents don't get any time on the bench. And although an aunt or grandmother might provide snippets of bench time once in a while, this isn't really enough. From time to time every parent needs to be completely out of the game, off the bridge of the ship, out of the battle.

"Sounds good," you might say. "But you don't get it. You're comparing ducks with sharks. I'm a mom twenty-four hours a day, seven days a week, three hundred sixty-five days a year, whether I'm there or not. You said so yourself. Being a mom is more like being the President than being a basketball player."

You're absolutely right. Being a mom or a dad is more similar to being the President than being a basketball player because no matter where the President goes, he or she is still the President and the problems are there. When he goes to Camp David for a weekend or flies in *Air Force One* to Paris or Tokyo, he's still in charge as the commander-in-chief. Wherever the President goes, his office goes with him. So do the telephones. And when there's an emergency, a disaster, misunderstandings with his staff, or tattling among his executive family, it doesn't matter where he happens to be.

"And that's how I feel as a parent. But I don't have an *Air Force One* airplane, sophisticated communications equipment, or a staff to help. And by the way, we don't have a fully equipped and staffed Camp David either."

All of these things are true. But you still need some time off. Parents need to escape from high-pitched voices once in a while to keep from going nuts. And you also need some time away from the kids to nourish your marriage, which is a very important part of being an effective parent.

START WITH A DATE NIGHT, THIS FRIDAY

So listen up! This is your assignment. You are going out on a date with your spouse—this week. And if you're single, you're going out with someone. The kids are staying home. It doesn't matter if you're out of money. It doesn't matter if you can't think of anyone to take care of the kids. It doesn't matter if you have too much to do. You're going out. Got it? But what if Friday won't work for some unchangeable reason? Well, if it's really an unchangeable reason then pick another night. And if you work nights, then do a date morning. Whatever. Just do it.

So get on the phone, or roll over in bed, or turn down the TV during the next commercial, and explain to your spouse about this Friday thing. Don't ask this time. Tell. Well, you'll probably use a little more diplomacy than just bluntly telling, but you can do it. You know how to get things that you really want. In other words, this is a basic need like water, so figure out a way and plan for your date this week, if not right this minute, at least before too many hours go by.

But we can't afford to go out!

I know what you mean. We've been there. But it's my contention that you can't afford not to go out. Of course, an evening out can cost lots of money. But my guess is that you've had some pretty good dates that didn't cost much of anything—maybe nothing.

Be creative. If you have a tight budget, find an inexpensive buffet or fast food place that you can afford. And if you really can't even do that, make some sandwiches and munch on them while you go for a walk. Borrow some bikes and go for a bike ride. Catch the metro or a bus. Go to a museum, an art gallery, or the zoo. If you can't afford tickets for a big league game, the symphony orchestra, a big-name concert, or a blockbuster live theater production, chances are there's a community theater, or a pretty good local high school play, chorale, band night, or ball game going on that doesn't cost much. Look around. You might be surprised by the events going on in your area and the places to go that could be lots of fun and are inexpensive.

But what about baby-sitters?

"Even if we figure out something really neat to do that doesn't cost much, there's still the problem of finding and paying for a baby-sitter."

Good point.

But if I gave you hundred-dollar tickets to something you really wanted to see, would you figure out a solution to the sitter problem? I think so. In other words, if you really want to figure out an answer to the sitter problem, you probably can. And yes, it is important to get a sitter you can trust. How do you do this? One good place to start could be recommendations from friends or neighbors. And how about grandparents, uncles, and aunts? And if you really can't afford to pay a sitter anything, you probably have friends who are in the same boat with whom you can trade kids so you can each have a date night out.

NOW DO THIS EVERY WEEK!
Once you've broken the ice and gone on a date with your spouse this week, do it again next week—and the next. You need more than a one-time tune-up! Setting aside one night a week, like Fridays, for a regular date with your spouse can become part of the week's routine. It will just happen. But if you have to stop each week and reinvent the idea each time one of you thinks it might be nice to take a break, weeks and months will slip by without doing it. I've seen this happen in so many families that I want to help you get out of this rut—or not let it become a rut.

There are dozens of reasons why you are too busy, too broke, or just don't get around to setting a regular date night with your spouse. But we're talking about your sanity. We're talking about your ability to cope. We're talking about you being a more loving person. We're talking about you being a more effective parent. Now do it. The assignment is not just to set up a date for this Friday night. That's just the first part. The second part of your assignment is to set up a date night for every Friday night, or another regular time if Fridays just won't work.

NOW GET AWAY OVERNIGHT!
I hope you're completely convinced to go out once a week on a date with your spouse. Going out on a date every week will be a

good beginning. But now I'm going to tell you that this isn't enough! Once in a while I think you need to get away, really away, on a little retreat—at least overnight.

Numerous times when I've suggested that a tired, discouraged mom get away on a retreat with her husband, the tearful reply has been, "That sounds nice, but I couldn't leave *my* children long enough to do that."

As I talked with Karyn, one of these tired mothers, who had brought in a sick youngster, I learned that she had been *on duty* as a mom for eleven years without ever having a real break.

After writing an antibiotic prescription for the child with the ear infection, I wrote another prescription—this one with Karyn's name on the top and the following instructions:

*Go on a little trip with your husband
and leave the kids at home.*

A little smile broke through Karyn's tears as she went on to explain all of the reasons this couldn't happen. But it did. A couple of weeks later I learned that she had figured out a way around the biggest obstacles—including overcoming her reluctance to leave the children. Obviously nobody could take her place. No one could do the job quite as well. But Karyn and her husband actually got away by themselves for the first time in years. They only ventured forth a few miles from home, but they had a good dinner and a quick overnight getaway in a nearby motel.

What about the children? Well, she found someone who handled things just fine. The kids didn't think Mrs. Perkins was all that great. She didn't do things like their mom. She was too strict. For one thing, Mrs. Perkins made them go to bed too early. Then they missed their mom's hugs after the lights were turned out. And they didn't like the cooked cereal she fixed for breakfast.

This little overnight outing for Karyn and her husband certainly wasn't very fancy—but it was great. She later told me that getting away that night was one of the best things she had done for her children. Even after being away just for one night, she felt much more like a human being than a robot. She was even happy to get back to her children. In fact, she could hardly wait. And the kids were happy to have their mom back home. Having Mom away was actually good for the children. They appreciated their mother more than ever. And getting away gives parents some peaceful, quiet time to be alone together—and intimacy in marriage is very important.

Three months later, Karyn and her husband took off for a couple of days instead of just overnight. They went to some shows, swam in the motel pool, and had time for themselves. And during the children's growing-up years, they got away on little outings like this a few times a year. In fact, when Karyn's husband got a promotion and was sent on an occasional company trip, she went with him when they could work things out.

* * *

If this sounds like something you need to do, here's the prescription—just for you:

*Go on a little trip alone with your spouse
and leave the kids at home.*

You can do it. Don't say you'll do it *sometime* and not really mean it. If you're thinking it would cost too much to get away, it's costing you peace of mind not to get away. If it's a question of who would take care of the children, I think you can figure this one out—grandparents, friends, or relatives can help.

You can probably find a nice place that's less than an hour from where you live. Besides helping you be more effective parents, getting away together will help bring some spark back into your marriage.

These little escapes make a big difference. Now do it. Don't just talk about it. Do it soon.

KEYS TO RAISING CHILDREN
1. **Take charge as a friend—not the enemy.**
2. **Make home a happy place to be.**
3. **Give your children something priceless— your time.**
4. **Don't say much until you listen.**
5. **Teach them the "rules of life."**
6. **Get help from your spouse or a friend.**
7. **Take time to regroup—away from the kids.**

8

Say More When Children Behave Well than When They Don't

re the things your children do wrong *biggies* or *teenies?*

having a messy room
throwing a tantrum
not wearing socks
eating junk food
using drugs
listening to obnoxious music
dropping a ball in a Little League game
stealing money from Mom's purse
leaving an overflowing bag of garbage
receiving a "D" on a history test
wearing a stupid-looking belt
getting into an accident after some drinks
wearing a crazy hairstyle
getting pregnant
shacking up with a boyfriend or girlfriend
dropping gum wrappers on the floor
leaving dirty dishes in the sink

licking a spoon that's then dipped in the ice cream
  carton
wearing grubby clothes
leaving a bike in the driveway
losing a library book
leaving homework undone

Some of these things are *biggies*.
Others are *teenies*.

These *teenies* could be *little teenies, regular teenies,* or *big teenies*. And the *biggies* could be *little biggies, regular biggies,* or *big biggies*.

WHAT ARE BIGGIES AND TEENIES?

Sometimes we get upset about *teeny teenies* like gum wrappers, or *regular teenies* like sloppy clothes, or *big teenies* like being a few minutes late getting home.

Then no one listens about the *biggies,* especially the *big biggies*. When you think about it, some of these are matters of preference. Others are matters of principle.

When it comes to your kids, do you get caught up in the little stuff or do you stay focused on what's really important? Most parents get trapped into fighting battles that don't matter and then run out of energy for the ones that do.

You can follow the simple principle that some things are *biggies,* but lots of things are really just *teenies*. If parents knew this they could save themselves lots of misery.

Which things are *biggies?* Which are *teenies?* This is something you need to figure out for yourselves. It isn't hard to recognize how much fuss most parents make about things that are not very important at all. Think. And when you do, you will be much less likely to "blow it" on *teenies*—or *biggies*.

WHAT IS REALLY IMPORTANT?

If this hits home and makes sense, you probably wonder how to know the difference between what isn't really important and what is, and where to draw the line. It goes back to principle and preference.

But even knowing this, sometimes it's very easy to get upset about relatively small things that kids do—like throwing gum wrappers on the floor. This doesn't mean that we should completely ignore things that make our home a mess. It's just that some of us get so intense when there's the least little thing that's out of place—that we need to have rules about these things without yelling and making everyone miserable.

CONSTANT CRITICISM TRIGGERS MORE MISTAKES

A certain negative coach always focused on the mistakes his team made during the game. A typical post game wrap-up included, "Look at all the mistakes you made. You gave the game away. That was the poorest performance I've ever seen. You didn't even try."

The morale of the team deteriorated. Being intolerant of imperfection, the coach seemed compelled to tell his players and the world about every error in judgment and skill. With constant criticism, even the star players began making more mistakes and they lost more games.

The fans, the press, and everyone else got tired of the coach's yelling, put-downs, and tirades. Eventually, the university fired the negative coach.

Even though I knew he had to go, when I heard on the radio that he had been fired a chill came over me. I felt sick to my stomach, even though I knew a change would help the team. It took me a few minutes to figure out why I had such an empty feeling. All of a sudden I realized that as a father I was just like the fired coach. When things didn't go right, I yelled at the kids and put them down, which was exactly what I didn't like about the negative coach.

Eventually, I figured out that my kids didn't do very well when I yelled at them about their mistakes. The more I focused on mistakes, the more mistakes they made. So I tried something different. I didn't do it as well as I would have liked, but when I started focusing on things they did well and talked about those things, I noticed a big change in attitude.

MISBEHAVING FOR ATTENTION

Behavior that attracts attention gets repeated. This is why it's a big mistake to tell a kid that he or she is *bad, mean, dumb, slow, sloppy, inconsiderate,* or anything negative.

But what if a kid is being bad or sloppy?

Don't put a label on him—as a person. The problem is the bad behavior—not being a bad person.

One of the things that helped me learn how behaviors reflect our comments was our success in creating a champion noneater. And over the years since, I've seen hundreds of little kids who were champion noneaters. In fact, I'm going to explain in detail how you can produce your very own champion noneater.

When a child in a high chair plays with his food and throws some on the floor as toddlers always do, first tell him that he is the worst eater in the world. This will encourage him to be an even worse eater, because children often become as they hear themselves described. If you tell a kid often enough that he's a lousy eater, a terrible passer, or a bad person, the label often sticks and the youngster will live up to it.

The next step in creating a real champion noneater is to beg and coax him to eat. Then when he doesn't, get visibly upset. The more attention you give the youngster for not eating, the more he will play with his food.

A toddler will then throw some peas on the floor. He will quickly become amused to find that one or more of the adults present will retrieve the peas. When he figures out that this is the most entertaining event of the day, he'll toss some more peas, maybe a few on the floor, a few across the room, and some under the refrigerator. This is even more fun because he then gets to watch a big person grovel on hands and knees trying to find the peas that have disappeared under the big thing with doors from which come milk and other things. You make the game more interesting by growing irritated, yelling, and generally becoming furious.

Then recruit a neighbor, aunt, or grandmother to come glare at the mess and to comment on how poorly the youngster eats. Pay lots of attention to the bad behavior.

When dad gets home, he can get into the act by becoming upset too, telling the youngster such things as how hard the mother worked to prepare the food, adding something about the starving children in Somalia.

Usually the grown-ups don't need much coaching to play their roles. They just do it by instinct. And as your toddler finds he can control the entire family by throwing his peas on the floor instead of eating them, you will produce your very own world-class *noneater.*

And it's all because of this simple principle: *Behavior that attracts attention gets repeated!*

When we focus on kids' mistakes—or on their bad behavior—it's very likely that they will keep doing it. Are you getting the picture of why kids do all sorts of irritating things—including picking on each other?

Whenever a couple of kids are together, one's going to push, poke, or do something to annoy the other. But why? It becomes a contest. The kid on the receiving end yells, "He hit me!" and the first kid yells back, "I did not" or "She hit me first."

This goes on and on, day after day, in most homes. Children receive lots of attention for their performances. Why would kids do things that make parents angry—and that gets them in trouble? It's part of the game. Children tease each other to trap a parent into giving them attention!

Don't get trapped!

The answer, although it seems ridiculously easy, is not to get trapped, not to yell at the kids, and not to run and see what's happening. So when a child comes and tells you a brother or sister is clobbering her, unless the situation warrants something more, give the youngster a little hug and continue what you're doing, without getting trapped into rewarding them for negative behavior.

"He isn't playing fair, and then he pushed me," a six-year-old reported to her mother about her brother.

"Your sister says you weren't playing fair," the mother parroted, looking at her son with a grin.

"But she pushed me first," the older brother protested loudly.

Maintaining her cool and keeping things light, the mom looked back at her tattling daughter and said, "Your brother says you pushed him first."

"I didn't, and he stuck his tongue out at me," the sister went on, trying a different tack to get her brother in trouble.

"Your sister says she didn't—and that you stuck your tongue out at her," the mom repeated, playing along with the dialogue to get the message to her children that the game of tattling and blaming each other wasn't going to accomplish anything. It worked—perfectly. Soon everyone was laughing at what was happening and the children ran off to play, the pushing and teasing long since forgotten.

But shouldn't I do anything about what they're doing?

When kids figure out that they don't get any reward for tattling and bad behavior, you'll be amazed by how much less teasing, arguing, fighting, and tattling occurs. You may question the word *reward,* but kids often do negative things to get your attention.

Most parents fall for it. But what if the kids are really hurting each other? If something dangerous is going on, put the kids in different rooms to cool off for a while or give them work to keep them busy. Remember, behavior that attracts attention gets repeated—and kids will often do foolish things to get attention—even bad and stupid things.

Pay attention to good behavior

Let's go back to the champion noneater. How do we change the noneater into one that eats? Start out with a big plate—a really big one, and put three peas on it.

"Three peas?" you may wonder.

Yes. Three peas and maybe a small spoonful of mashed potatoes and half a spoonful of something else. Then when the child tosses one pea on the floor and eats one, smile and tell him he must really like peas!

"For eating just one pea?"

Think about it. Since behavior that attracts attention gets repeated, he might eat another pea—and a little of something else. This changes the focus from being a champion noneater to the success of eating two peas and a little spoon of mashed potatoes. It's the same principle as a coach commenting when a player catches the ball instead of yelling when it is dropped.

If you're worried that a couple of peas and a little potato isn't enough nourishment, keep in mind that toddlers don't need as much food as you may think. And if they're hungry, they'll certainly eat!

But after the first little servings are gone, put a little more on the plate. These small servings are not as overwhelming as a mountain of food. So sit back and relax. Kids will eat all they need—if they don't fill up on snacks and if you don't make them stars for not eating.

Why teens do outrageous things

Would you believe that older children and teenagers act very similarly to toddlers? Have you ever wondered why teenagers wear outrageous clothes? They wear these grungy, awful outfits to irritate their parents, to please their peers, and to be accepted. And this is also why a teenager may show up with green hair, long hair, short hair, or striped hair.

"But why would kids want attention for doing foolish things?" you may still wonder.

They want the attention, just like the little child. It doesn't make sense. But listening to outrageous music, drinking, smoking, or other negative behaviors get the attention of other kids—while showing adults that the child is in control.

Everyone needs attention

By the way, it isn't just kids that do things to attract attention. To some extent everyone wants to get attention for something—even grown-ups. Some do it by becoming very good at their work. Others sing, raise flowers, train horses, paint portraits, play the piano, run marathons, go out for the basketball team, or write poems—while others try to get attention by doing all they can to become thin and beautiful.

FOCUS ON STRENGTHS—NOT ON WEAKNESSES

Life is tough for kids. Sometimes even school is scary.

Instead of ten football games to win or lose in a season, a kid has around 182 days of school every season—each one of which can be won or lost. Kids are not going to win every game—or every day. Knowing that our kids are going to get lots of put-downs, we should be sure we don't add to the put-downs.

Don't ever tell a kid he's dumb, she's lazy, or . . . he's a lousy eater.

One of the most important things a parent can do is build on a kid's strengths. Every kid has strengths. Build on these strengths. Talk about them. Say more about a kid's strengths than about his or her weaknesses.

My heart goes out to kids when a coach, or teacher, or parent concentrates on weaknesses.

"LEARNING PROBLEMS"

There's a special concern when children have a problem learning. Before parents realize what's going on, people may think the child with a problem like this is stupid or lazy.

You probably know about a boy who was thought to be *addled*—which today some unwisely term *brain-damaged*. That so-called addled boy, whose teacher didn't want him in her classroom, was Thomas Alva Edison. The word *addled* has long since been retired. So should the term *brain-damaged*. No child should ever hear this expression in reference to himself.

But back to the addled Tom Edison—among his many successes, Edison failed in ten thousand experiments to invent the incandescent light. However, instead of considering these failures, Edison realized that he had found ten thousand ways that didn't work.

Tests often miss strengths

Essentially every child and adult alive has some weaknesses. And every person has strengths as well. Unfortunately tests are geared to check certain strengths while they completely miss many others. Thus in today's world of tests and more tests, some very capable kids are screened out of many of the so-called best opportunities in life.

There are lots of kids today who are really smart, but like Tom Edison, they don't do very well in school. And unless someone helps them understand their strengths, they believe that they can't do anything because they have been told there's something wrong with their brain.

In our society, these strengths are often overlooked and

missed. Every time youngsters turn around there's a test—spelling tests, math tests, language tests, pop quizzes, midterms, finals, oral tests, written exams, driving tests, ACTs, MSATs, LSATs, IQs, and achievement tests.

Some children, and some grown-ups, almost never do well on tests. Others always do well. Even the ones who do well can have a bad day. Sometimes one test may determine whether doors are opened or closed—and may determine a kid's whole future. And the best test is only a tiny window into the mind.

When a parent emphasizes a child's strengths and helps compensate for weaknesses, children with *learning problems* often do very well. Don't let anyone convince your child that he or she is inferior.

EVERY KID CAN DO GREAT THINGS

Not every kid can be a great quarterback—or a math whiz. But every kid can be somebody. Every kid can do great things.

One of a parent's biggest jobs is to help a youngster discover his or her strengths and then reach his or her potential. Sometimes these talents are hidden. But parents open the door for opportunities.

If we look for weaknesses in children, we'll find them.

And if we look for strengths in children, we'll find strengths.

In a world where the emphasis is to look for mistakes and weaknesses, parents instead need to look for strengths and help a child build on them. As kids look to us for direction, we can give them confidence.

Try to look past the *teenies* and your kids' weaknesses—and build on strengths.

BE A CHEERLEADER

One of the most important things we can do as a parent is to be a cheerleader. Kids need someone who believes in them, someone who will be on the sidelines cheering about what they do right. They need someone who will keep cheering even when they drop the ball.

In *The One Minute Manager,* Ken Blanchard and Spencer Johnson taught us to catch people doing something right instead of catching them doing something wrong, which most of us do so much of the time. In Spencer Johnson's later books, *The One Minute Father* and *The One Minute Mother,*[15] he suggests that if we can't catch kids doing something right, to catch them doing something *approximately* right. Here's a snippet from Dr. Johnson's story about a fictional father who didn't like his son's attitude: "He decided if he waited until his son did something perfectly right, he might have to wait a very long time. So he decided he would catch his teenager doing something *approximately* right."

Most of us can catch our kids doing things right more often than we do—and everyone can catch kids doing something *approximately* right. Now we need to do it and tell them about it.

REPEAT COMPLIMENTS AS OFTEN
AS COMMERCIALS

An article about effective marketing in *The Wall Street Journal* explained that successful companies convince people to buy their products by repeating short messages hundreds or thousands of times in radio and television commercials. Hearing or seeing an ad once or twice isn't enough. This is why we need to continue cheerleading our kids over and over, emphasizing their strengths with sincere, honest compliments. It's important to be sincere and truthful. Focus on the good stuff, not the things that are not so good. And remember, *behavior that attracts attention gets repeated.*

If we sincerely repeat compliments to our children about their strengths and good behaviors, some of it might soak in—

[15] Spencer Johnson, M.D., *The One Minute Mother* and *The One Minute Father* (New York: William Morrow, 1983).

like repeated commercials. You have a tremendous opportunity to help your kids set their sails. If a youngster knows you believe in him or her, it will make a huge difference in everything this kid does in life. Unfortunately the world is filled with competitors, put-downers, and even enemies dressed up to look like friends. Sometimes even teachers, counselors, and other professionals plant doubts and discouragement in the minds of kids. So it's up to you.

* * *

You can and should be your child's strongest advocate. I don't mean to excuse or cover up mistakes or to be an enabler for bad behavior. I don't mean taking over responsibilities that belong to your youngster. But I do mean that as an advocate you need to know what's going on at school. You need to know if a kid's teacher yells all the time, is completely unfair, or is otherwise out-of-bounds. And if this happens, you need to be tough enough to do what needs to be done about it—often behind the scenes.

You need to be your kid's public relations person. You need to be your youngster's coach about life—along with being his or her loudest cheerleader. This means believing. It means encouraging. It means finding your youngster's strengths and building on them, constantly and repeatedly. And, of course, to do all these things means being careful not to mess up your relationship by constant picking out *teenies* that really don't make much difference in the big picture.

EXAMPLES OF THINGS NEVER TO SAY TO CHILDREN:

> Can't you ever do anything right?
> You mess up every time you do anything.
> Why can't you ever throw a ball straight?
> You're an outright liar.

You're as obnoxious as your father.
You are just plain mean.
Why can't you be more like your brother?
You sure are a brat.
Why do you always pick on your sister?
Why don't you ever get your work done?
You're the most irritating person I know.
Why are you always so bad?
You are the laziest person I know.
You sure are dumb.
I can't believe you're so stupid.

EXAMPLES OF COMPLIMENTS TO GIVE CHILDREN SINCERELY (BEING CAREFUL NOT TO BE PATRONIZING):

That's a great picture. Tell me about it.

I wish every dad was lucky enough to have a daughter like you.

I just want you to know I love you.

I've never seen anyone work as hard as you've been working.

That's a terrific report.

I'm pleased you figured that out.

You're really good at solving those problems.

I have lots of confidence in you.

You always have had good common sense.

I know you can do it.

You really think about the important things in life.

A kid who can do this is going to be a big success.

Your smile is your trademark.

You did that better than I could have done.

You're really bright to have thought of that.

Somewhere there's a boy who deserves a girl like you.

Thanks for teaching me that.

You've always been our peacemaker.
Thanks for taking care of this.
You're a real leader in our family. We appreciate that.

KEYS TO RAISING CHILDREN

1. **Take charge as a friend—not the enemy.**
2. **Make home a happy place to be.**
3. **Give your children something priceless— your time.**
4. **Don't say much until you listen.**
5. **Teach them the "rules of life."**
6. **Get help from your spouse or a friend.**
7. **Take time to regroup—away from the kids.**
8. **Say more when children behave well than when they don't.**

9

When Children Make Mistakes, Give Miniscoldings, Minipenalties, and More Love

---

B
esides all the other hats you wear, you are a judge. In fact, you're also the jailer, legislator, jury, governor, prosecutor, detective, witness, and law enforcement officer.

If this sounds more like a banana republic dictatorship than a family judicial system, it's because in a family parents fill all of these rolls. Sometimes it seems you can't change from your police person suit fast enough to get into your judicial robes and then back in the jury box.

Justice. Mercy. Fairness. Learning. Forgiveness. Due process.

You probably didn't take a course called "Law and Justice in the Home" any more than I did. Suddenly, we just find ourselves filling these rolls.

FIFTH AMENDMENT RIGHTS

If there were a course called "Law and Justice in the Home," one of the class sessions should be on the application of the Fifth Amendment in the home. The Fifth Amendment says that you don't have to testify against yourself.

This is a pretty good law in the courts of the land because it means that the law enforcement officers and prosecutors have to prove to a jury that someone's guilty—without requiring the person to be the source of the evidence used against him.

Somehow, Fifth Amendment rights are often forgotten in home law when children are the suspects. *Okay, who did it? Tell me what you did. No dinner till you confess.*

I think you've got the picture. None of these questions is fair—that is, in a court of law you can't make someone testify and incriminate himself or herself. In families, we do it all the time.

So what's the big deal? Families are different. Yes, they are. But there is a problem with backing a young child or teenager into a corner to ask him if he did it. When backed into a corner, if a child admits to a family crime, he or she knows it means big trouble—often a big penalty.

This creates an enormous temptation to lie. *I didn't do it. Oscar did it. The dog ate my homework.*

One of the last things we want is to have our children tell us untruths. Lying may be even worse than the crime. And getting away with a lie, which sometimes happens in family home law, multiplies the problem—because it teaches a youngster that it's possible to get away with something wrong by lying about it.

The point is that I really want to be able to trust what kids say. So although some of what I said about Fifth Amendment rights in a family was somewhat facetious, I'm serious about doing whatever we can to discourage outright lying in order to avoid detection and punishment.

PRECONFESSION IMMUNITY

Since family justice isn't exactly based on court law, here are some suggestions. First, if at all possible, figure out the guilt or innocence of a childhood offender without calling on him to testify against himself. If this isn't possible, and no other solid proof reveals that a youngster is guilty, and if it's necessary to question a youngster about a particular offense, be very careful about how you ask the questions. On many occasions I granted preconfession immunity for telling the truth. In other words, I let the kids know that, to me, telling the truth was so valuable that for absolute honesty, penalties would be waved.

Exceptions

Now, there are circumstances when giving immunity for a confession may not be the right thing to do. In criminal law, a person who commits a crime such as burglary or perjury can't expect not to go to jail by admitting the crime and saying, "I'm sorry." Some crimes and misdeeds in society, or in a family, are so serious that they shouldn't go unpunished—whatever the degree of honesty after the fact.

But for lesser offenses in a family, telling the truth and the embarrassment of guilt may be sufficient penalty. On the other hand, if a youngster tells the truth about a minor offense and gets a severe penalty, there may be an incentive to bend the truth the next time. Honesty is very important. However, in our judicial wisdom we need to be very careful not to allow a youngster to take advantage of the principle or to manipulate the situation.

HANDLING KIDS WHO AREN'T QUITE PERFECT

Well, besides this short course in Griffin law, I have two reasons to be confident about being able to help you deal with kids who aren't quite perfect. First, I made lots of mistakes. Second, so did our kids. Thus we have lots of experience in dealing with mistakes.

There are many ways to handle children when they misbehave. Some are very effective. Others are not. Remember to be a friend instead of an enemy. This is as important in arriving at justice as it is in teaching values. If we consider a youngster an enemy, it's very difficult to be fair. And if a youngster considers us as enemies, then whatever we do won't be perceived as fair.

It's unwise and unfair to investigate, prosecute, judge, or administer penalties when we are angry. No matter what kids do—no matter how bad it is—they deserve a fair hearing, a fair evaluation, and a fair family justice process. And it's hard to be fair when we are angry, especially if we are out of control. So, whatever else is going on—and I'm speaking from experience—cool down before you proceed with any judicial process in your home.

Be fair.

There are several advantages to having swift justice. But more important than being swift is being fair and doing the right thing. Mistakes by parents in family justice can be very damaging. This is why one of the significant keys to raising children is, *when* they make mistakes, to give miniscoldings, minipenalties, and more love.

MINISCOLDINGS

A miniscolding—what's that? A miniscolding[16] is a very, very brief scolding. Condense the chewing-out part of what you need to say into one brief line. Then look your kid right in the eyes and firmly say something like, "It makes me very angry when you don't come home on time. We worry about you."

While you continue looking the offender in the eyes, don't say anything for another twenty seconds or so. Take this time to think of something nice to say. Then, sincerely and softly say something like, "You know, I really love you."

All this takes less than a minute. You may wonder how you can possibly scold anyone effectively in a minute or less. Well,

---

[16] The concept of the miniscolding is based on the principle of the one minute reprimand presented in *The One Minute Manager* by Kenneth Blanchard and Spencer Johnson.

you can. Usually, a miniscolding has greater effect than going on and on about what happened.

No long speeches

When a youngster does something wrong, it's natural to want to tell him what he has done wrong again and again. I've certainly been guilty of this many times. In fact, I was terrible about expressing my displeasure and saying the same thing again in another way. Some of my lectures to kids rambled on for twenty or thirty minutes instead of the twenty or thirty seconds we've been talking about in a miniscolding. Can you imagine getting yelled at or lectured to for thirty minutes or more? It would be awful. I wouldn't like it—and neither would you.

Once, when I was giving my daughter one of my famous long speeches, she interrupted me saying that I had given that speech so many times before that she could give it herself. She went on to suggest that I number my speeches and when I was upset I could just give the number—like 34-C—instead of the whole speech, and she would know exactly what I wanted to say without saying it! This was pretty smart because by the time I said, "Okay—speech 34-C," we were both laughing, which diffused my anger—and she got the message.

After that, when I was quick enough to think about it, instead of giving a long lecture about something kids did wrong, I'd say a number, like speech 34-C or speech 16-B; it broke up the tension and the kids seemed to get it. Kids almost always know exactly what they did wrong and how we feel about it—so we don't need to give a big speech. Anyway, miniscoldings are more effective.

Almost anyone can handle a miniscolding. No one can tolerate being berated over and over for something. So after a miniscolding, that's it. The lecturing is over. If the misbehavior isn't serious, the penalty is over too. Quit while you're ahead.

What if the misbehavior is serious? What if a kid has done

something to warrant some other punishment? Often letting a youngster know he or she has disappointed you is enough— especially if you really express your love in the last part of the miniscolding. Try it. You'll be amazed by what happens. A youngster who expects a long lecture will really think about what you say in only a few words.

Your principle strategy

Miniscoldings are so effective that I suggest using them as your principle disciplinary strategy. But even though miniscoldings are very effective, sometimes when a youngster is out of control, talking isn't quite enough. Sometimes you'll want to throw in another kind of play—like a minipenalty. But if miniscoldings are so good, why do anything else? Well, if a football team only has one play, it won't work for very long. To be effective, a football team needs lots of plays—a good passing offense and a good running game. Without a passing offense, the defense can focus on defending the run. Without the ability to run, a passing offense isn't likely to be very good either.

So whether it's parenting or football strategy, you need depth and options. An excellent system of family discipline includes miniscoldings and minipenalties. With balance, you'll find these strategies will be very helpful. They work.

MINIPENALTIES

Minipenalties are very short punishments imposed to interrupt obnoxious behavior or to make it very clear that a particular action is not acceptable.

They are something like time-outs, but are usually shorter and more effective. For a very young child, an hour or even a half-hour time-out is quite a long time. And like groundings for older children, imposing a penalty that's too long can backfire.

Next time you need to stop a negative action, or impress a youngster with the idea that what he said will not be tolerated, try a three-and-a-half minute minipenalty.

Try a three-and-a-half-minute minipenalty

"A three-and-a-half-minute penalty?" you may be wondering. "What good would that do?"

Just try it. You may be surprised. Minipenalties can be extremely effective.

Think about what you're trying to accomplish when you punish a child. You want the youngster to learn to obey the rules—and eliminate unacceptable behavior. The purpose of a punishment is not to be mean or get even, but to teach rules. Actually, a better word for what we're trying to do is *discipline* not *punish*. A minipenalty interrupts disruptive behavior like talking back, mouthing off, or throwing a temper tantrum.

"So if a child has been rude to you, how do you impose a minipenalty?"

Compose yourself and in your softest voice, say something like, "That is totally unacceptable. To help you remember not to say that again, sit on the wood stool in the laundry room for three minutes."

Use a timer

As you announce the number of minutes for the penalty, set the length of the penalty on a little kitchen timer. It will help you keep track of the time. The timer also makes things seem *official*—the mechanical gadget now controls the time instead of you. As the timer clicks away, it may even deflect some of the hostility that may have been directed at you. Especially if placed where your child can see and hear it, the timer may reduce the protests that the *time is up* and repeated questions like, "How much longer do I have to sit here?" And the ticking away of the timer adds a little to your mystique and judicial wisdom.

Don't lecture during minipenalties

Although it may be tempting, there are some good reasons why it's best not to give a lecture about inappropriate behavior during a minipenalty. In fact, the less you interact with the offender during this time, the better. This is not a time to argue. Let the effect of the penalty soak in. As your child sits there and thinks about what has happened, he or she will learn a much better lesson than a long scolding would teach. So let the timer tick away without saying anything. Don't even let him know you're looking at him. Just get out of the way and let justice prevail.

Use add-ons

"But what if a kid yells out another insult?" Add another two or three minutes to the minipenalty. And if the tirade continues, add a couple more minutes.

When you're dealing in minutes and fractions of minutes, these add-ons or extensions are manageable both for you and the youngster. Remember, the point is to stop the action and provide a deterrent—not set up a home prison.

In deciding how long to make a minipenalty, be creative. Make it interesting. An effective minipenalty may be for as little as two minutes, but it can break the momentum of the negative behavior. Try varying the length of the minipenalties, depending on the seriousness of the offense.

Keep penalties short

Remember to keep the penalties short. For one thing, you may have to add on time and you don't want the total penalty to go on for more than a few minutes. Coming up with the right number of minutes for a penalty is part of the art of parenting, especially if you throw in a penalty that has a fraction of a minute—like three and a half minutes.

Giving a youngster a three-and-a-half minute penalty gets her to stop and think, "I wonder how she came up with that number," especially if another time it's two minutes even—and another it's four and a fraction.

As you keep a child guessing, she will think you're pretty smart. A kid will wonder how you came up with such an odd penalty. She will think about what she did and try to figure out why this time the penalty was a little different from the last one. So besides the break in the action of the negative behavior, you are getting the kid to think—which is exactly what you want. Using minipenalties will help you maintain your cool and stay in control.

Give them a work detail

You can also have children help you with housework or other chores during their penalties. We have lots of weeds around our place and pulling weeds for a few minutes makes an effective minipenalty an even more effective deterrent. If you don't have weeds, you probably have something else that needs cleaning— a basement, garage, storeroom, yard, sidewalk, or gutter. You might as well put kids who are old enough to work while serving their minipenalties.

Use minipenalties for temper tantrums

Almost every parent has had frustrating and embarrassing experiences in dealing with temper outbursts when a youngster doesn't get his way. Since a child usually throws a tantrum to manipulate a parent into giving him something, a minipenalty is usually a good way to handle the temper tantrum—even when he seems capable of screaming louder and longer than any kid in town.

But parents who don't know how effectively a swiftly administered minipenalty can manage tantrums will try to talk kids out of them. They often ask or tell the youngster to be quiet. When this doesn't work, they warn a child that she will be sent to her room if she doesn't stop. But the youngster seldom listens or stops screaming. At this point the parent usually gets more upset and the encounter escalates.

As most parents eventually discover, begging, coaxing, or threatening a youngster having a temper tantrum never works. In fact, getting you upset is part of what the misbehaving youngster wants to accomplish. She's punishing you for not giving her what she wanted. This is Manipulation 101. The kid is controlling the entire situation.

So what do you do? No negotiating. No rewards. Decide ahead of time that there will never be any rewards or benefits for manipulative activity—not even attention, because as you know, *behavior that attracts attention gets repeated.*

When a youngster pitches a fit, impose a minipenalty—right then. Simply pick up a toddler and gently and immediately whisk her off to the penalty area, saying little if anything. How long should a minipenalty be for a tantrum? That depends, of course, on the age and the circumstances. But the idea of a minipenalty is to keep the confinement short—a few minutes or until the youngster stops yelling, when you can explain you love her so much that you have to do this anytime there's a tantrum.

Use minipenalties for teens, too

By the way, we've used minipenalties for kids of all sizes— sometimes even teenagers! Among those who have laughed at this outrageous idea was a person who asked skeptically, "How do you get a big kid to sit on a stool—or to pull weeds for seven minutes?" Try it.

One of our big, tough teenage sons said something rude to his mother. Now this kid was big enough to pick me up by the scruff of the neck. But I looked right at him and said, "Since you chose to say that to your mom, sit on this chair and think about it for four and a half minutes."

"You can't do that to me," he protested.

"I just did," I replied.

"But that's what you do to the little kids," he snapped back.

"You're acting like a little kid," I answered.

When he threw something at me in disgust, I added six more minutes. He thought about all of this as he sat there, and got the message.

It probably would have been even better to have had him pull weeds. Four and a half or even ten-and-a-half minutes isn't a very long weed-pulling session, but it's long enough for a kid to do lots of thinking. A few minutes may not seem like a very big penalty, but to a kid you are taking minutes away from his freedom.

A minipenalty like this can diffuse a difficult situation. And sometimes there's an advantage to the wheels of justice grinding swiftly, and getting the problem over and done with quickly.

If an older youngster tells you that he isn't going to do something you have asked him to do, you may decide to assess a seven-and-a-half minute penalty to think about it. Or for using bad language, you might think that he deserves fourteen minutes or longer if the profanity is directed at you.

Use minipenalties instead of grounding

I don't like groundings. They are not as effective as miniscoldings, minipenalties, and taking away specific privileges for limited periods of time.

Groundings are also difficult to enforce and parents are easily manipulated—which teaches kids that they can get out of things. Besides, groundings often backfire.

"When I grounded our son for a week, my wife got soft after two days and let him off," a father told me. The situation became compounded for many reasons.

Another family I worked with had a big problem after the dad grounded his teenager daughter for two weeks when she had come home a little late from shopping at the mall with a friend.

She was not permitted to go anywhere except to school—

which she thought was very unfair. The mom became the guard and jailer—which grounded her as well as the teenager.

As the days passed, the girl became more and more hostile. When she found out she couldn't go to a school dance she became so angry that open rebellion began.

Even if the offense had been slightly worse than coming home a little late, grounding a teen for two weeks is a tough sentence for the kid—and for the parents. Instead of teaching how to do something better, a long grounding penalty almost always creates resentments that can cause more negative behavior.

In this case the kid snuck out the window, which made the relationship between father and daughter even worse. Another teenage girl was so rebellious about being grounded that she climbed out of her bedroom window in the middle of the night, crawled in her boyfriend's window, and spent the night with him. If grounding solved problems or changed behavior, it might be worth providing locks, controls, and guards to be sure a grounded youngster didn't get away.

Another reason I don't like grounding is that I want our children to enjoy being home. I don't want them to think of home as a prison. In fact, as I mentioned earlier, home should be a happy place to be.

* * *

Minipenalties are short and manageable. Seven minutes pulling weeds in the hot sun isn't any fun but it gets a point across. A minipenalty isn't cruel. When handled properly, it teaches a lesson by taking away a few minutes while expressing love. It's amazing how well minipenalties can work, even when a child is incorrigible and otherwise unmanageable.

Extending the penalties a few minutes for ongoing rants and raves, or for calling you a jerk, is much more manageable than doubling a two-week grounding to four weeks. Once, when I gave a nine-year-old a seven-minute minipenalty, he responded by calling me a dummy. So I quietly said, "That just cost you four more minutes." It's surprising how well minipenalties work. They are like being put in the penalty box during a hockey game.

Although it's easy for a parent to make an error in judging and sentencing a youngster, when we are dealing in two-and-a-half and six-minute penalties, it's hard to make a very serious mistake.

When a minipenalty is over, be sure to tell a youngster that you love him. Make it short—not a long, syrupy speech, but something like, "I love you so much that I had to help you learn not to say things like that" or, "Thanks for sitting there obediently. I love you and want you to be happier than you can be when you choose to do that."

The effectiveness of minipenalties multiplies when both parents use them regularly.

TAKE AWAY PRIVILEGES

If a teenager comes home late, you might consider deducting the amount of time she was late from her next curfew. So if a teen shows up at one in the morning instead of midnight, without a very good excuse, she has to be home by eleven the next time she goes out. Or if the offense is a little more serious, you might take away the privilege of going out at all the next Friday night.

Another effective penalty instead of a lengthy grounding for a minor infraction is simply to assign an hour or two of extra chores. Along with extra chores, you might take away telephone privileges. You'd be surprised by how effective it is to take away the telephone for two hours. Teenagers hate not being able to use the phone, even for a short while. Prohibiting incoming and outgoing calls for an hour or two creates a real impact. It's a reasonable way to give a strong message without causing more problems.

If an infraction is repeated, you might prohibit phone use for longer than an hour or two—maybe three or four hours, or on occasion for an entire day. But in general it's usually a good idea to keep penalties short.

Another privilege you could take away for a while is television. Even if a youngster had not planned to watch anything for the couple of hours you ban it, if a kid can't do it, that's exactly what he or she wants to do.

So we're talking about a minigrounding for a teenager and sometimes for younger kids. An hour. Two hours. Maybe three hours of no phone, no television, no friends. It may not sound like much of a penalty to you, but it can be very effective. And it's enforceable.

The more you try the simple principles of miniscoldings, minipenalties, and taking away specific privileges, the more I think you'll like this strategy. You'll feel more in control. Will it work perfectly all the time? Of course not. But these techniques help to avoid situations that provoke children and teenagers to rebel even more because they are scolded and punished. And miniscoldings, minipenalties, and taking away privileges do provide ways to teach kids that there are consequences for misbehavior.

SPECIFIC MISDEEDS HAVE CONSEQUENCES

Whatever a youngster's age, it's important to help kids realize that there are consequences for misdeeds. Here's an example concerning a young child—but the principle applies to transgressions for kids of all ages. When a mom noticed that her five-year-old son, Frank, was chewing gum on the way home from the store, she knew he didn't have any money to buy gum, and figured out that he had picked it up at the store along with a candy bar he was hiding. Since Frank was already chewing the gum, his mother explained that he would have to earn the money to pay for it. Frank worked for the next hour cleaning the front hall closet and the bathroom.

This gave the boy a chance to learn that you have to work for what you get. His mother paid him for the work, and on the way back to the market she explained that whether or not you're caught after doing something wrong, you feel terrible.

When they got to the store, the manager thanked Frank for returning the candy and paying for the gum. The manager also told Frank about an older boy who had been arrested for shoplifting and was now in jail. The manager was friendly but firm.

Missing money

When kids get away with stealing, it encourages them to do it again and again. Unfortunately a common problem in many families is having money disappear from around the house—especially from a mom's purse or from places where other children keep their money. Even when parents suspect that a youngster has stolen money, it is often very difficult to prove. Kids will often compound their crime by swearing up and down that they didn't take the money. This is a serious problem.

But there's more to this than losing the money. Parents have a major responsibility to teach children not to take money or property from anyone. And if kids get away with stealing money from parents or each other, they will do the same thing at school and in society.

Honesty is one of the important lessons we must teach our children. If they don't learn it at home, they will learn it the hard way where the consequences may be getting arrested and having a juvenile record—or even worse.

Stealing money at home is a major problem. But parents also need to be careful about credit cards because sometimes kids will "borrow" a parent's credit card and go on a shopping spree.

When one mom and dad had a problem with vanishing money, and each of the children denied taking it, they marked some money and left it where it could be found. Although the parents didn't like playing detective, they made tiny marks on the paper money with a pen and hammered three dots on several quarters.

To recover the money, they asked to borrow some money until the next day to pay for a pizza. When some of the marked money appeared, they confronted their son with the evidence, told him they loved him, and set some appropriate penalties. But more important than the penalties, the dad took his son on a tour of the county jail and helped him find a job so he could earn enough money to pay back his brothers and sisters. The happy ending is that this boy grew up to be a man of integrity and trust who now has several sons of his own. This is certainly a good example of effective parenting. But it also reveals how difficult it is to be a parent.

Shoplifting

"The police just called to say my son has been caught shoplifting," a worried mother told me on the phone.

This was a tough situation—one that's all too common. Parents can't help but be disappointed. It's easy to become so angry that the unconditional love we are supposed to have often may not come through. This is not a time for anger, lectures, or yelling. Instead, if something like this ever happens in your family, let your kid know that you love him. No matter what else is going on, a kid who has broken the law and is arrested needs lots of love and support.

Parents need to be there. It's not a kindness to a child who has committed a crime when parents manipulate the system. If the charges are serious, it's wise to get competent legal advice. But parents should not get kids off the hook to keep their record clean. When this happens, instead of learning not to break the law again, a youngster learns that there is a way out and is more likely to get into trouble again. The moment the law is broken, a child's record is not clean. When parents use power, influence, and money to get a kid out of a jam, the youngster learns that someone else will take care of things, relieving him or her of the responsibility. When parents truly show love but let the law proceed on its natural course, there is usually less likelihood that the lawbreaking will reoccur.

Destruction of property

Another kind of trouble kids too often get into is the willful destruction of property—at school, in the neighborhood, or even at home. Why kids would break windows or paint graffiti on buildings, buses, or subways, or do any other kind of damage, is difficult to understand. Most of the time vandalism occurs when kids without something better to do get together with other kids who don't have something better to do. Sometimes the motive for vandalism is to gain acceptance by a group or gang, retribution about something that doesn't seem fair, or to feel in control of something.

If the damage is at home, it might happen when a youngster has become angry at a parent because of a punishment or perceived unfairness. In a rage of temper, this otherwise good youngster may do something stupid, like punching a hole in a door or wall with his fist.

When a youngster damages property at home or anywhere else, the kindest thing a parent can do is to help him learn that mistakes have consequences. The natural consequence for painting graffiti or maliciously breaking windows must include the youngster paying for the damages—not the parents. Hard work must be part of the restitution.

Likewise, if a youngster punches a hole in a wall at home, it means repairing the hole or working to earn enough money to pay for the repair. If the child can't do the repairs himself it may also be a good idea to give him the job of arranging for and paying a handyman or drywall contractor to do the repairs.

Breaking driving rules

If a teenager breaks family driving rules, a young driver should lose the right to use the car—for a reasonable time—in addition to paying any fine imposed for breaking the law. Parents should never "fix" tickets or pay children's fines.

Some parents have their teenagers sign a contract about the right to drive in exchange for them signing the papers for the teen's learner's permit—with the understanding that drinking, drug use, or breaking driving rules will result in forfeiture of the right to drive for a period of time.

SERIOUS MISBEHAVIOR

Hopefully your youngsters will never get into serious trouble. But sometimes a youngster from a good family with good parents gets into big trouble.

Sometimes a child, especially in the teen years, really disappoints us. When this happens, it's important to love the kid while disapproving of the behavior. This is not easy to do. But no matter what kids do, they need us to love them.

If a kid who's made a mistake thinks that we hate him, turning things around is much more difficult. The skill in parenting is to be able to teach the lesson without losing a youngster.

How?

Be calm. The next time you have a big problem with a kid, try talking slowly and softly to get the message across: "I'm on your side. I'm your friend. I'm not your enemy." Instead of yelling or giving a long angry speech, try a miniscolding.

Remember, the goal in discipline is to change behavior. Sometimes we have to be tough. But love is the most important part of effective discipline. The more that kids make mistakes, the more love they need.

Sometimes disappointing you, embarrassment about what has happened, and the natural consequences of the misdeed are sufficient punishment. Other times, some privileges need to be taken away. You don't want to err by being too tough or by being a pushover either.

Problem friends

"What do you do when a kid starts associating with friends who are a bad influence and who do things that you completely disapprove of?" a worried mother asked.

You and I can't pick our children's friends. We can try, but it usually doesn't work. Most of us would be quite content to let our children pick their own friends—if they would pick ones who are a good influence and won't get ours into trouble.

This question focuses on a major problem. It's a vicious cycle because running with certain friends will put them in places and situations that are going to get them into trouble. The best solution is prevention—which goes back to being a friend and not an enemy, so that a kid feels like you're on the same side.

Do what you can to discourage a youngster from spending time with peers who are trouble. Let him or her know you care. Take the kid on a trip. Go out to dinner together. Listen. Talk. Think through every possible thing you can do and say. Keep cool. Don't make things worse.

Extend privileges when better choices are made. Encourage the kids to spend time at your place. Make them feel at home even if they have weird earrings, grungy clothes, and hairstyles that don't meet with your approval. Don't compromise principles about drugs, alcohol, smoking, inappropriate videos, or sex. But try to make your home a gathering place where kids will want to bring their friends.

NEVER GIVE UP

All kids mess up once in a while. Hopefully your kids won't do anything very wrong. But if one does get into lots of trouble, focus on and build on his or her strengths more than ever. A kid in trouble especially needs a parent who believes in him or her. This doesn't mean excusing behavior. There must be consequences. Besides taking away the use of the car and other privileges, be sure you are not an *enabler*—particularly for drug and alcohol use. Don't supply money. Don't do anything that would make it easier for them to drink, use drugs, or break the law. But it's important to get past the goof-ups—and to look ahead.

Whether a youngster is bugging everyone at home with a terrible temper, has cheated in school, started a fire, been drinking, tried drugs, run away, stolen a car, or become pregnant—the important thing is to give love unconditionally. Any of these things is upsetting. Some are easier to handle than others. But there is a way back even after serious mistakes.

Helping a kid turn around who has been in trouble may take a long time. It may be very difficult. Don't expect everything to change right away or in a matter of weeks or months. It might. But sometimes it takes years. And sometimes we have to measure progress in decades. That's why Winston Churchill's advice is so important: "Never, never give up."

No matter how bad things are, there's always hope.

With this in mind, when kids mess up, and they will, don't make things worse. It's tough to make good parenting decisions—so work together at it, especially when there are big problems.

Remember *three-step problem solving:*

1. Get together privately.
2. Think together.
3. Make the best decision you can.

And . . .

> play with them
> give them advice
> enjoy them

laugh with them
hurt with them
work with them
listen to them
talk with them
teach them
make suggestions
and love them, whatever they do

NO ONE WINS EVERY GAME

It's quite natural for parents to feel crushed, down, discouraged, and disappointed when youngsters make poor choices and do not live up to their expectations. Sometimes kids will wear things we don't like. Sometimes they will annoy others in the family. Sometimes they won't do what we ask them to do around the house. Sometimes they will choose music we don't like. Sorting out the preferences and principles is really important. Unfortunately, sometimes children, and particularly teens, choose things that are exactly opposite from what will bring them long-term happiness.

It's no fun to watch your favorite team lose a game. But a team very seldom wins every game. Only one or two major college football teams in the country go through a year with an undefeated record. And when they do, it usually doesn't take long the next season before somebody beats them. The same is true with our families. I'm sure you don't like to lose games any more than we do. Think of the times the best quarterbacks throw interceptions and the receivers drop the ball. I certainly don't like to drop the ball, but when it happens it doesn't do any good to brood about the mistake. It's much better to learn what we can and keep going.

STICK TOGETHER

When you or your spouse gets down, try to help the other one be happy. One of the best ways you can do this is to be happy yourself. It makes a big difference. When children and teen-agers create problems, parents often become frustrated and distant.

It's easy to blame each other. When things go wrong we often think, "If you had just . . ." or "If I had only . . ."

"If's" are not real. And it doesn't help to keep looking back, re-running the video replays on life. If there's ever a time when we need each other for support and love, it's when kids go astray.

Even people who love each other may not feel much love or intimacy in the midst of the trials of parenting. That's all the more reason for parents to get away from time to time and do whatever it takes to rekindle courtship.

BE SUPPORTIVE

Remember that one of your main jobs as a parent is to be a cheerleader. Being a cheerleader in your family is more impor-tant than being a critic, more important than being a penalty giver, and more important than almost anything else you can do.

You can be an inspiration to each of your children. You can coach a youngster into feeling like a winner.

Here's how to do that:

- Give millions of honest compliments.
- Say the right things at the right times.
- Learn not to say the wrong things.
- Believe in your youngster when no one else does.
- Look for strengths and build on them.
- Love your child even when he or she misbe-haves.

It takes parents to raise a child. Being a responsible parent takes lots of commitment. It also takes lots of work. Remember, these are your kids and they are your responsibility—not the state's, not some expert's, not the community's and not even the school's.

No one can take your place. If you don't teach them, there's a good chance no one will. It really does take a parent to raise a child—best of all, two responsible parents.

It won't be easy, but I'm confident that with the skills you've already acquired and these nine keys, you'll continue to be more and more effective as a parent. You can do it and I know you will.

KEYS TO RAISING CHILDREN

1. **Take charge as a friend—not the enemy.**
2. **Make home a happy place to be.**
3. **Give your children something priceless— your time.**
4. **Don't say much until you listen.**
5. **Teach them the "rules of life."**
6. **Get help from your spouse or a friend.**
7. **Take time to regroup—away from the kids.**
8. **Say more when children behave well than when they don't.**
9. **When children make mistakes, give mini-scoldings, minipenalties, and more love.**

LOOKING AHEAD

All of a sudden it will be ten years from now. Turn around again and your kids will be grown.

Between now and then you'll have lots of adventures. There will be some really good days and good seasons, along with some lousy ones.

Among your frustrating problems, your kids will probably have ear infections, lice, allergies, skirmishes with friends, misunderstandings with teachers, their bicycles stolen, speeding tickets, car wrecks, and other problems that will make you and them miserable. And while these things are going on, you'll also cope with broken water pipes, washing machines that self-destruct, increasing taxes, stresses at work, job changes, and other crises that will try all the patience you can muster.

When your youngster makes mistakes, it will be heartbreaking. But you won't give up—ever, no matter what. Somehow you'll make it through whatever tough times come along.

Happiness is watching your kids get things right. But this won't happen without lots of tears too—sometimes over little everyday things and other times over some big, big problems.

Being a mother is the toughest job in the world.

Being a father is the next toughest.

You're a parent twenty-four hours a day, seven days a week, all year long. When you climb into bed at night, or go on vacation, the responsibilities and worries are still there.

You can handle almost anything—money problems, cleaning grease off the carpet, changing diapers, getting a call about trouble at school, or trying to get a wayward kid back on track. The overload comes when all these problems hit you at the same moment, and then another phone call brings you more problems.

You can only be in one place at a time. You can only solve one problem at any particular instant. So line things up in the order of importance and take care of one thing at a time.

This means that some things are not going to get done. So do what you can, let your kids know you love them, and then give yourself an "A+."

By the way, it's okay to give yourself a little compliment now and then. From time to time, most people talk to themselves, saying critical things like, "That was really stupid," or, "You're an idiot." If you've been doing this, stop. Instead, tell yourself things like, "Good going," or, "You handled that really well!" Then, when things don't go so well, don't scold yourself or beat yourself up about things you might have done better.

It's impossible to make the right decision every time, but my guess is that you are right 87.4 percent of the time—and that's good in any league.

Very few families are spared serious problems with their children. The more you know about families, the fewer you will find who don't have a current crisis going on at any one time.

But over the next few years, your children will have numerous successes. They'll learn to work. They'll learn to be honest from the lessons you teach them and from real-life experiences. Your children will learn to follow the "rules of life" because you love them enough to teach them these time-tested principles. So even with the bumps you'll hit along the way, you'll know you're doing a good job as a parent.

Besides planning and following through on one-on-one activities with each child, you'll take time to take care of yourself—to let your mind settle, to have some fun, and once in a while to escape from the kids to regroup.

On one of these escapes, I'd like you to think about a friend of mine, Kimbal Warren, who lives across our little country road at the mouth of Hobble Creek Canyon. Besides being a famous Western landscape artist, Kimbal is a rugged but gentle horseman. You'd have fun watching Kimbal talk with his horses. He's a horse whisperer.

Kimbal spent more than a thousand hours training his gray, and more than two thousand training his chestnut. With patience, kindness, attention, consistency, lots of stroking, and a hug now and then, horses bond well to their friend—trusting him so much they rely on his common sense and direction even on narrow trails high in mountain country. He always shows his horses respect and his horses respect him.

Yet, even with all this respect, attention, love, trust, and bonding, once in a while Kimbal's chestnut still acts up—testing the limits to see how much he can get away with.

If you had the chance to listen to this soft-spoken man or the original horse whisperer, Monty Roberts,[17] you'd be amazed at what you'd learn about training horses—and children.

After observing herds of wild mustangs on the range and learning how they communicate, Monty cut a colt from a herd. On horseback, he stayed close to this wild mustang for several days and nights. When the colt dashed off, so did Monty. When the mustang stopped, so did he, careful to give the young horse plenty of breathing room. They became constant companions. The horse whisperer didn't rush things. He was patient and quiet—occasionally breaking the silence to talk softly with the wild horse. Then Monty turned away, letting the colt feel safe enough to want to turn and follow, which is exactly what happened.

Slowly, confidence turned into trust and with this trust the wild horse bonded with this unusual man. Little by little, the

---

[17] Monty Roberts, *The Man Who Listens to Horses* (New York: Random House, 1997). More information about Monty's program to train horses with gentleness is available on the Internet Web site: *www.Monty Roberts.com.*

mustang was willing to accept a saddle—then a halter and other tack. Monty's secrets with that young horse, and with thousands since, were patience and respect.

Traditionally, *breaking* a horse has meant force. Tight ropes, harsh commands, chains through the mouth, sack coverings, spurs, whips, and kicks—all to break the will and dominate the young animal. Kimbal Warren and Monty Roberts don't do these things. No chains. No whips. No hitting. No kicking. No forced restraints.

They don't *break* a horse. A horse whisperer *starts* a horse. This involves trust and confidence—not force or pain. A round corral is used so that the horse won't feel trapped in a corner. A young horse is allowed to run because he must have plenty of breathing room and know that his trainer is not an enemy.

At the right time, the trainer moves in close, listening to what the young horse is saying by the way he positions himself, sets his ears, and moves his body. The horse whisperer establishes eye contact with the young horse—sending a message of trust and confidence. After a while the trainer looks and turns away—an invitation for the horse to follow voluntarily, which, as with that first time on the range, he almost always does. What a contrast there is between *breaking* and *starting* a young horse.

Of course, after being *started* properly, a colt has hundreds of other things to learn. And this takes time—lots of time. It isn't surprising that a young horse does much better with patience and repetition, and with teaching instead of telling.

Raising children is much like training horses. It takes being there without hurrying. It takes giving respect before you expect to receive it. It takes listening. It takes knowing when to be quiet. It takes building confidence and trust—gently. It takes lots of work. It takes repetition. It takes letting them run the open range. It takes staying with them and keeping them in sight—without making them feel pushed or crowded.

It also takes understanding that even after being trained, children will test their limits. It also takes understanding that children, like horses, will revert to old habits without an ongoing investment of individual time and attention.

I hope you will become a *child whisperer* as you love and work with your kids. Gain their confidence. Pay attention to them. Talk softly. Make it easy for them to come to you. Treat them with respect. And just love them. Then remember that whether it's horses or children, success is measured over the long haul, not at the end of a day, a school year, or any other point in time.

After the years have flown by, one day you'll sit back and realize just how fortunate your kids are that you have been their parent—a *child whisperer.* And more than ever, you'll know: *It takes a parent to raise a child.*

ACKNOWLEDGMENTS

I was fortunate to have been born to very good parents, each of whom spent lots of one-on-one time with me while I was growing up—and in the years since. Mom and Dad did lots of listening, teaching, coaching—and even more cheerleading. We were best friends. But they cared enough to be *lovingly firm.* They were tough. When it came to principles, there was never any question about what was right and wrong. So thanks, Mom and Dad—this book is a tribute to you.

I wish everyone could have a marriage partner and parent for their children who is as loving and wise as Mary Ella. She has been the right balance when I've been too tough. She's been the anchor and a helpful mom when I was too busy with patients or something else I thought was important at the time—but really wasn't. Our life has not been a fairy tale. We've had some tough times—some really tough ones. But, if we had it to do all over again and were choosing up sides for our family, Mary Ella would be my very first choice of anyone, anywhere, to be my partner and the mom for my children.

And talking about our six children, each one is absolutely precious to me. Each has taught me things I would never have learned otherwise. I hope they will forgive me for the mistakes I made along the way. Incidentally, recognizing these mistakes and sharing them with you makes this book worth more than all the ivory-towered theories you can find. So thanks to Jan, Joan, Mark, Gary, Jill, and Greg. My love and appreciation is greater than you can possibly know. And thanks to the spouses of our children—and to each of our very special grandchildren.

Another person deserving top billing for this book is Lara Asher, my editor at Golden Books. Lara is one of the two best editors I've ever worked with as an author. While fixing things that need fixing, it's a big temptation for an editor to rewrite a book, changing the flavor and even the meaning of what the author is trying to say. Instead, Lara helped make what I wanted to say even clearer—without making the writing sound like someone else. So thanks to a great Golden Books team: Lara Asher; Laura Yorke (Golden's senior editor and Lara's excellent coach); Jennifer Prior, my copyeditor; and Gwen Petruska Gürkan, the art director.

In today's publishing world, it takes an agent who believes in you to get a book published. But getting a literary agent is not exactly like finding an agent to sell you life insurance. What a happy day it was when Gareth Esersky called to say she loved the book and was sure she and the Carol Mann Agency could get it published. Thanks, Gareth and Carol, for many suggestions that made the book better—and for believing.

From their perspectives as moms and educators, my sisters, Janet Lee and Lois Jenson, gave me many, many helpful suggestions in the text—and Janet thought up the title.

My friend Dr. Rick Parkinson helped fine-tune the manuscript, adding a couple of great stories to drive home points.

Countless others also helped—patients, parents, friends, newspaper editors who ran my parenting column, and good people who knew how to make the manuscript better, I especially want to thank Pauline Torgersen, Jan Lee, Kitty Musser, Ed and Marie Bak, Claudia Larsen, Jeanne Redfield, Pam Blaisdell, Mike and Michelle Baer, Drew and Tamra Kriser, Mark and Jennifer Griffin, Bob and Jan Selover, Jill and Greg Nord, Gary Griffin, Michael and Sharon Lee, Diana Allred, Ben and Marian Griffin, Joan Watson—and, of course, Mary Ella.

Oops! This may sound like an admission that it took a village to write this book about not raising a child by committee. Well, I did need the help of many—just like you'll need all the help you can get in being a parent. But just as the responsibility of what's in this book is mine, the responsibility of raising your child is yours—not a village's.

ABOUT THE AUTHOR

Glen C. Griffin, M.D., is a well known pediatrician, writer, and co-author of the best-selling book *Good Fat, Bad Fat*. He is the coordinator of pediatric education at the Utah Valley Family Practice Residency. Dr. Griffin is also president of the American Family League, a nonprofit foundation that provides resources on its Web sites, *www.principles.org* and *www.moviepicks.org* such as suggestions for movies and videos that are *entertaining* and *decent*—and clues for families about Internet safety. The American Family League also presents the prestigious Ginny™ Family Values Award to recognize exemplary family living, principled teaching, and those who create particularly outstanding and wholesome motion pictures, videos, books, and other creative efforts.

Dr. Griffin is a member of the National Advisory Board of the Medical Institute for Sexual Health, which created national educational guidelines for teaching character and sexuality. Prior to being appointed editor-in-chief of *Postgraduate Medicine,* one of the world's leading medical journals, Dr. Griffin was a family pediatrician, counseling parents and caring for countless young children and teenagers for almost three decades. Always seeking ways to improve the quality and comfort of care, he designed and built a no-waiting-room medical clinic so patients could park in front of, and come directly into, their own exam rooms that looked and felt like small living rooms.

Besides serving in leadership positions in charitable, church, and professional organizations, Dr. Griffin has prepared educational materials that have been used internationally. He is a popular speaker with an engaging style, quick wit, and helpful answers.

Dr. Griffin and his wife, Mary Ella, live in Mapleton, Utah, and have six children and fourteen grandchildren.